The

PHILOSOPHER'S

TOUCH

●

EUROPEAN PERSPECTIVES: A SERIES IN
SOCIAL THOUGHT AND CULTURAL CRITICISM

EUROPEAN PERSPECTIVES

***

A Series in Social Thought and Cultural Criticism

Lawrence D. Kritzman, Editor

European Perspectives presents outstanding books by leading European thinkers. With both classic and contemporary works, the series aims to shape the major intellectual controversies of our day and to facilitate the tasks of historical understanding.

For a complete list of books in the series, see pages 167–168.

The

PHILOSOPHER'S TOUCH

●

SARTRE, NIETZSCHE,

and

BARTHES

at the Piano

François Noudelmann

TRANSLATED BY BRIAN J. REILLY

Columbia University Press
New York

Columbia University Press
Publishers Since 1893
New York   Chichester, West Sussex
cup.columbia.edu
Le Toucher des philosophes: Sartre, Nietzsche et Barthes au piano.
Copyright © Editions Gallimard, Paris, 2008
Translation copyright © 2012 Columbia University Press

Cet ouvrage publié dans le cadre du programme d'aide à la publication
bénéficie du soutien du Ministère des Affaires Etrangères et du Service
Culturel de l'Ambassade de France représenté aux Etats-Unis.

This work received support from the French Ministry of Foreign Affairs
and the Cultural Services of the French Embassy in the United States
through their publishing assistance program.

Library of Congress Cataloging-in-Publication Data
Noudelmann, François.
[Toucher des philosophes. English]
The philosopher's touch : Sartre, Nietzsche, and Barthes at the piano /
François Noudelmann ; translated by Brian J. Reilly.
p. cm.
Includes bibliographical references.
ISBN 978-0-231-15394-2 (alk. paper) — ISBN 978-0-231-52720-0 (ebook)
1. Sartre, Jean-Paul, 1905–1980—Knowledge—Music.   2. Nietzsche,
Friedrich Wilhelm, 1844–1900—Knowledge—Music.   3. Barthes, Roland—
Knowledge—Music.   4. Music and philosophy.   I. Title.
ML79.N6813 2012
780'.01—dc23
2011033876

Columbia University Press books are printed on permanent
and durable acid-free paper.
This book is printed on paper with recycled content.
Printed in the United States of America

c 10 9 8 7 6 5 4 3 2 1

Designed by Lisa Hamm

CONTENTS

1   Intuition • 1

2   The Off-Beat Piano • 7

3   Why I Am a Great Pianist • 49

4   The Piano Touches Me • 95

5   Resonances • 145

Acknowledgments • 157

Index • 161

The

PHILOSOPHER'S
TOUCH

●

One

INTUITION

My inspiration for this book came from watching a video of Jean-Paul Sartre playing the piano. The scene takes place in 1967, a time when this writer-philosopher is engaged on all fronts of international politics. He has been traveling the world lending support to revolutionary struggles, holding discussions with the likes of Castro, Tito, Khrushchev, and Nasser. Since 1945 he has become a man of incendiary declarations. Threatened with death by the defenders of an *Algérie française*, he is also feared by de Gaulle. At the Russell Tribunal, he had judged the Americans for their crimes, and now they have him under surveillance. Yet, in the middle of this militant and adventurous euphoria, Sartre routinely set aside time for himself at the piano. Not in order to play the notes of the *Internationale*. No, instead he would sit down to sight-read scores by Chopin or Debussy. I was taken aback by this discovery: Having spent many years studying Sartre's texts and thought, I was now hearing another—and wonderfully unique—voice from him. He expressed so much of himself in the way he played a piece, in his approach to the instrument, in how he held his fingers and moved his body. It was not so much the discovery of Sartre the pianist and music lover that surprised me—he had already spoken of his taste for music in *The Words* [*Les mots*]. It was, rather, the sight and sound of a man producing another rhythm, a rhythm that was so different from the one we hear in his public speeches or voluntarist writing.

Still, let us not imagine that another, hidden Sartre suddenly emerges here as an exceptional performer of the pianistic repertory. We would only laugh at the astonishing clumsiness with which this insatiable amateur played, all the while aware that he was being filmed. Sartre had practiced playing the piano since childhood and would continue to do so until the very last years of his life and the onset of his blindness. Had he been capable of performing Bach or Schumann brilliantly, it might have given us some insight into this "supplementary" pastime of so polymorphous a man who managed to invest just about every domain he entered with high culture. Instead, his way of not playing while still playing, of glancing at the notes with both carelessness and understanding, of playing at once stiffly and passively, testifies to a temporality and a corporeality. Simply put, it testifies to a life, or, as he would have said, to an existential mode. In the video, Sartre is with Arlette Elkaïm, his adopted daughter, and the camera breaks into their intimacy—although Sartre, a believer in transparency, never feared flaunting his private life. Still, we would be led astray were such an analysis to encourage our voyeuristic indulgence. Indeed, the power of this historical document resides not in any insight we might find in a rather staged scene of private life, but in the experience it gives of a unique duration and unique rhythm.

Making music and playing music both engage the body in complex postures and temporalities. Roland Barthes discovered how to approach this phenomenon by distinguishing the act of writing about music from that of playing it. He observed this distinction through his own experience, for he too was a passionate amateur pianist. He sensed the peculiarity at play in playing an instrument: An instrument engages its player in a different way from social codes. One's choice of instrument—the piano rather than the accordion, for example—is not, of course, unimportant. Nor are one's tastes, even if they remain confined to the repertory typical of bourgeois living rooms. Still, underlying the sociology of musical practices, there are tempos, pulsations, personal and unexpected touches. Certain philosophers—like Rousseau, Adorno, Jankélévitch—have been able to tie these unique moments together by speaking learnedly about the music rest from their writing desk. All were music lovers and musicians themselves, able to reconstruct scholarly discourses from their experience as performers, or even composers. For them, temporalities were thus united: Their music and their discourses harmonized. Not so for Sartre, who wrote almost nothing about music. He restricted his own playing to moments outside of intellectual discourse and thereby allowed himself brief and melodious moments of escape. The word *melody* might seem strange here in reference to Sartre, who was usually so quick to break the well-ordered etiquette of the social score. Melodies, however, were indeed what he liked to sing and play.

The musical tastes we reveal in public do not always correspond to those we hold dear when alone. Sartre wrote on Xenakis and Stockhausen but loved Chopin, just as Nietzsche wrote about Wagnerian modernity but wept while playing mazurkas. Barthes's beloved composer was Schumann. Romanticism, which had so enlarged the piano's range and power, remained the music of choice for these three pianists, even if they preferred to discuss their (nearer) contemporaries in public. Overly hasty critics see this as proof of an antimodernism too shameful to admit to in public. Nevertheless, such incongruity tells us much more than any mere contradiction, for rather than something contrary, it exposes a secret, a negotiation, a suspension. It reveals a different side not only of these writer-thinkers, but also of ourselves.

The unity of the self is a construction that hides the personal dissonances and rhythms with which we never cease to compose. And playing an instrument, far from expressing who we are, engages us in the experience of an active passivity and a different time. My choice of these three writer-philosophers—Sartre, Nietzsche, and Barthes—comes from my interest in temporality as a window, an opening onto the self as subject to compositions. The piano is assuredly not the only path to free oneself from the collective rhythms of society. Nevertheless, playing the piano is no simple hobby, no mere *violon d'Ingres*. I believe, through my own long experience with this instrument, that it engages a unique disposition to the world, to past generations, and to the contemporary. Among the signs confirming such an intuition, I note that the musical activity of these three thinkers often contravened their public works. The discordances thus revealed allow us to approach this gap and take a step to the side. We can observe the unchaining of the will and the play of the body that result under the constraint of touch and tempo.

The connections among these three thinkers cannot be limited to analogies between their lives. Instead, we find a proximity between them that exceeds discourse. Nietzsche had suggested using a tuning fork to evaluate philosophies and existences. With this vibration-inducing hammer he sought to strike philosophy's grand abstract constructions and to make what was in them resonate, revealing either a bass drum or a subtle string. By using such small, revealing strikes, I try in this book to capture what distinguishes these three music lovers. Their lives and ideas overlap in unexpected ways, and we can hear them in dialogue and debate with each other under the radar of History. The pieces they played more or less amateurishly made them quiver with vibration in return, conducting their bodies toward different rhythms. In this way, they created unique modes of relating to time, pleasure, the will, and friendship. When playing the piano, this trio composed, in ways discrete and active, the philosophical contours of their thought.

Two

THE OFF-BEAT PIANO

Was Sartre interested in music? To establish the range of our probe, we can begin by perusing the many studies that he devoted to the arts, including *matiériste* painting, kinetic sculpture, photojournalism, popular cinema, African poetry, the American novel. His works present a near encyclopedic repertory. Almost nothing escaped Sartre's drive to capture what was new. An insatiable curiosity lies at the bottom of his conception of the total intellectual, someone authorized to speak about everything, beyond any disciplinary specialization. There was no need to be an artist or a historian to write seriously about art: Intellectuals, on principle, get involved with what doesn't concern them. This definition of the intellectual applies to a physicist concerned with the military use of her discoveries, but it also authorizes the layman to claim all that interests him. The sociology of intellectuals teaches us that such an extension of discourses favors the growth of a symbolic power. The bonds woven between philosophers and artists augment their respective legitimacy and field of action. Thus many plastic artists circulated within the Sartrean constellation—Masson, Giacometti, Calder, Wols, or Rebeyrolle—just as earlier avant-garde artists had clustered around intellectual figures like Breton. Such federations seem to have a harder time, however, incorporating musicians.

Sartre wrote only belatedly about the music of his own century. He discovered Schoenberg and became interested in serialist aesthetics thanks to René Leibowitz, the composer and theorist who made the twelve-tone technique (dodecaphony) widely known after the war. But it wasn't until the 1970s that Sartre wrote more generally about the modern composers who were at the heart of contemporary debates (Stockhausen, Xenakis, Boulez, Berio). And then there he was, once again in the flow of obligatory references used by intellectuals to position themselves in public debate. He had earlier defended writers like Blanchot, Sarraute, Genet, and Ponge, before they had become established. Now he could discuss the physiology of sound, electro-acoustic material, mathematical formalism, and aleatory games. He editorialized, making distinctions among composers and incorporating ever more of the contemporary avant-garde. Decidedly omniscient, this Sartre had, from very early on, a will to know everything, to miss nothing of his own century. During these later years, he wanted to maintain the upper hand because now he was fighting against those who would render him obsolete—structuralists and *nouveau roman* authors who, on Foucault's account, made him out to be a man of the past, a "philosopher of the nineteenth century."

In 1978, as the basis for some interviews with him, Michel Sicard and Jean-Yves Bosseur had Sartre listen to a few records of contemporary music. These interviews allowed him to put the finishing touches on his reflections on music, for this philosopher had since become a musicologist, all other artistic fields having already been covered. To be sure, Sartre could speak about music more than other intellectuals by reason of his own musical culture and practice; he had played the piano since childhood. Not every philosopher knows how to read a musical score: Rousseau, Nietzsche, Wittgenstein, Adorno, Jankélévitch—they were exceptions. Sartre could uncover the cellular writing of Stockhausen and unravel the pieces of Messiaen. He was capable of reading them, playing them, performing them. Yet what a mistake it would be to picture him doing so! When Sartre was alone at the piano, he played Chopin far more readily than any avant-garde composers. We could imagine that, like any amateur used to his instrument, he was just occasionally practicing all of the repertoire learned in his youth. But no: Sartre played Chopin assiduously, again and again without end!

Those of a diplomatic bent will say here that one can love both Romantic and atonal music, just as one can appreciate Delacroix as well as Mondrian. More sectarian minds will cry foul: Chopin is like Renoir, and Impressionists are good only for wrapping or lining boxes of chocolates! Ridiculous! Why not Gounod or Bizet while you're at it! Ah yes, Bizet. There were, after all, some troubling precedents—Nietzsche had been compulsive in his adoration for Bizet's *Carmen*. Yet we refuse to believe it: Surely that hammer-wielding philosopher was just being provocative. It's just not possible for Nietzsche to have so praised Wagner and also embraced Bizet!

Sartre's case gets worse when we learn that he also listened to comic operas. When he wished to impress his own audience, one of his favorite numbers to play was the tune of the "Roi de Thulé." Sartre would play it from a transcription of *Faust* while singing at the top of his lungs. What could seem more out of sync with his learned commentaries on the mathematical language of avant-garde music! As Adorno warned us, culture dies when grand airs are sung in the shower or whistled in the subway. And yet Nietzsche loved to hum melodies, and he criticized Wagnerian music for not being able to be whistled due to its unnerving modulations. Further provocation? The matter is getting ever more complicated, and our usual guideposts are becoming obscured.

How are we to explain such a gap between listening and playing, between public discourse and private pleasure? Is it imposture? contradiction? dissonance? a secret conservatism? The reality is less clear-cut. More interesting for us is to follow this path of escape through which one's synchronous self can become disoriented with unsuspected rhythms. In this gap, in this path of escape, we can see a complex movement develop in the relation of a subject to the intersection of different times: chronological, historical, and singular. These debates cannot be reduced to questions of taste or to some imagined compatibility among musical genres. Instead let us ask what happens when an intellectual like Sartre retreats from the noise of this world to play Chopin. How do those who profess themselves to be abstract thinkers experience emotions, the body, and touch? How do they find themselves implicated and disconcerted by these feelings, these movements, and these durations of time?

If we have difficulty imagining him playing pieces of Romantic music, it would be even more incongruous to think of Sartre as a Romantic himself. Everything pits him against self-complacency, tearful sentimentality, or the grandiloquent solitude of the misunderstood. And yet. . . . And yet Sartre was not insensitive to Chopin's world, to that interior landscape composed of the images, sounds, feelings, and postures of the Romantic musician. After all, didn't Sartre often project himself into personalities that were otherwise quite removed from him? Baudelaire, or Genet, for example. And, of course, Flaubert. Sartre both loved and hated Flaubert throughout his life—from his childhood, in which he was troubled by the mischief of Emma Bovary, to his old age, when he stubbornly set about writing thousands of pages on this brilliant yet insufferable bourgeois. Would not Chopin too constitute similar temptation? Would he not be for Sartre an impossible incarnation, one barely avowed but persistent throughout Sartre's performance of his musical works? Now, however, there would be no need for some grand treatise on an author. Instead, everything would pass tacitly through the tips of his fingers.

When Sartre played Chopin's preludes, he put on a cloak of soft melancholy, draping himself in fading light. A controlled dizziness would glide into his body. These pieces of music carry with them the climate of their composition, and Sartre knew well the reveries attached to each score. He has fun with them, playing them half seriously, half sarcastically—as an actor caught up in his own imagination. The preludes send him off to Valldemossa, carrying him toward the place this tubercular composer chose for his exile. There, unbeknownst to his friends, Chopin would secretly meet up with George Sand. Hidden away in this charterhouse on Majorca, Chopin composed music while the energetic writer Sand went off to survey the island, no matter the weather. She might smoke a few cigars on the cliffs, quarrel with some narrow-minded Majorcans, or even sometimes confront the very storms and winds coming off the sea. During this time, Chopin looked for his blue note. He was in the throes of the *zal*—a Polish word for an evening melancholy. He suffered from this melancholy and, at the same time, cultivated it. It was winter, damp and muggy. Sartre too knew this climate, with its kind of fog that goes to the bone, as can be found in La Rochelle or Le Havre when the sky is low and heavy with rain. But the sublime unleashing of the elements did not procure any ecstasy for Sartre; nor did the terror of the steep slopes, nor the vegetal outpourings of nature. And when his own writer-companion, Simone de Beauvoir, would take him out through the deepest heartland of France, he preferred to rest at the foot of some mountainous peak. Sartre would write pages and pages on nothingness, while de Beauvoir, the Beaver, trudged around. Even if our image of him remains as a rock impermeable to all weather, Sartre knew well how one's mood could be porous to the surrounding climate.

The hagiography of famous men tends to hide their depressive and melancholic moments. But the playing of music gives focus to these moments, prolonging them as much as it produces them. While composing the preludes at Valldemossa, Chopin recalled to mind his childhood friendships and remembered his friend Tytus, whose brotherly sweetness he yet missed. Chopin's throat was becoming ever more phlegmy, constantly congesting his tuberculosed lungs. This is, no doubt, the very image of the Romantic composer, at least from an ironic point of view. But Sartre was not altogether without empathy for such a condition. He shared a taste for morbid and indecisive states of mind even long before he began to write learnedly on the phenomenology of the viscous and the phlegmy. At the age of seventeen, he published a short story that had as Romantic a title as one could wish for: "The Angel of Morbidity" (L'ange du morbide). It recounts the fascination its protagonist, a professor, has for the world of sanatoriums. Sartre projected himself into this detestable character, who was meant to be the incarnation of bourgeois hypocrisy, maintaining appearances only to better hide his perversions. The ambivalence between disgust and fascination is sustained through the story's romance involving the perverted protagonist and a woman with tuberculosis. The professor is a windbag who delights in his love's loose coughs, at one point exclaiming: "I love a consumptive, it's a consumptive I love, the one I love is consumptive." The young Sartre's suspicious insistence on condemning his character discloses his own, personal attraction to morbidity. The scene in which the professor attempts to kiss his consumptive love inverts the traditional motif of kissing a leper. This bit of daring features, first, a phlegmy lapping sound and, then, a spitting up of blood. The frightened professor flees, fearing he has been contaminated.

The true contamination has taken place in Sartre's own imagination, which takes in the oneiric pathologies of Romanticism. But this Romantic vein was then covered over by a taste for abjection, the very mark of existentialist literature, in favor of an antibourgeois realism. We can see this in the change in title of *Nausea* [*La nausée*], which replaced Sartre's first choice: *Melancholia*. And we might forget that, in Sartre's prose début, a Luciferian angel of melancholia presided over the phantasmagoric visions of a disenchanted world. Sartre's own closeness to Chopin is not, therefore, limited to the Romantic piano but can also be seen in the disenchantment of a solitary man alone in a world of collapse. Whether played out or mocked, these aspects of Romanticism were shared by Sartre. Through the theme of tuberculosis, indeed even through that shopworn cliché of a composer's blood-stained handkerchiefs, Sartre's empathetic imagination was on display. As the setting for his story of a tubercular-loving protagonist, Sartre had chosen Alsace, the homeland of his maternal family, the Schweitzers. Yet it was on the paternal side of his family from the Perigord that Sartre had similar feelings for his beloved cousin, Annie Lannes. A consumptive, she died at the age of nineteen. Sartre nevertheless had time to introduce her to Paul Nizan, whose death in 1940 would deprive Sartre of an irreplaceable friendship. For a time, Annie became part of the Sartre–Nizan duo—the fusional couple dubbed Nitre–Sarzan—and even gave her name to Roquentin's lover in *Nausea*. Much has been said of the trios involving Sartre, de Beauvoir, and whichever adopted mistress of the hour. And we've gossiped about the genuineness of this formula, which oscillated between open relationship and perverted duo. But these dangerous liaisons *à la* existentialism have hidden the intimacy Sartre shared with Nizan in his youth—an intimacy rather incompatible with our usual iconography of the militant couple of Sartre and de Beauvoir. Sartre's choosing to introduce Koch's bacillus into his masculine friendship with Nizan suggests a conspirator's fascination for sick flesh and morbid ecstasies. Tuberculosis is a way of expressing one's love through a contagion at once physical and sentimental. It recapitulates, in fact, a desire experienced by Sartre when he was quite young for André Bercot, a classmate at the *petit lycée* Henri-IV. Bercot was a brother to Sartre, for he had also lost a father. In *The Words*, Sartre confides that he loved Bercot, who was "handsome, frail, gentle" with "long, black hair combed in the style of Joan of Arc." But, at the age of eighteen, he too died from tuberculosis. This illness became a sign of election, uniting sensitive souls while contaminating nature. On a metaphoric and poetic level, the tubercular temptation Sartre experienced never ceased to haunt his landscapes of choice: Naples, for example, whose grimy secretions he wrote about, with its sickly streets sweating putrefaction; or, of course, Venice, both Tintoretto's Venice and the one he saw from his window in the summer—spongy, like a lung engorged with water. Sartre's depictions thwart any touristy glorification of his beloved Italy, preferring instead this entangling of the human with suffocating miasmas.

Readers of Sartre might have difficulty believing that some pianistic empathy had led him, an experienced philosopher, toward tubercular contagion and maudlin music. They recall perhaps the scathing passages from *Nausea* about how the provincial bourgeois give themselves over to facile, posturing states of mind when listening to Romantic melodies. Roquentin's aunt Bigeois, for example, consoles herself after the death of her husband by listening to Chopin's preludes, but he mocks her, noting: "The concert halls overflow with humiliated, outraged people who close their eyes and try to turn their pale faces into receiving antennae. They imagine that the sounds flow into them, sweet, nourishing, and that their sufferings become music, like those of the young Werther; they think that beauty is compassionate to them. Dumb fucks." Roquentin is the ruthless Sartre, hard and clear, disdainful in his disillusionment as the solitary man—a man who won't be fooled. But there is also a playful Sartre at work here: When he sat down to the piano, this young antihumanist writer sustained, between comedy and temptation, both his solitary tempo and his personal fantasies. Sartre always kept these ineffable moments at a remove from his all-consuming polygraphy. This man who wrote about everything, who never stopped filling pages upon pages to describe what he was living, thinking, wanting—this same man kept the piano outside of his writing. The playing of music escaped his will to tell all, to understand all. No doubt such an exception arises less from some secret or from a cuddled private life than it does from a kind of time—a time that resists analysis and defies being put into words. Playing this instrument is an activity unlike any other: at once outside and yet, nevertheless, there. So let us now observe Sartre at the piano; let us look at and listen to his fingers, which have been freed from their usual conscription to the pen and lined page.

From his refuge on the rue Delambre, Sartre is playing the Nocturne in G minor, op. 15, no. 3. A mist has invaded Montparnasse, and rain is drizzling on the wet rooftops. He is sixty-two years old; those cheerful walks with Nizan over the bridges of Paris are far in the past. He nevertheless partakes in the intimacy of a young, delicate woman, away from the hubbub of the boulevards. Arlette sometimes accompanies him, at other times listens to him play.

Chopin's nocturnes regain their bel canto melody that the two imbue with a sorrowful languor. It is a melody that the amateur allows to linger, without being rushed for time by others. Music lovers allergic to Romanticism cannot stand these prolongations that seem to emphasize minor dissonances and modulations beyond reason. But Sartre is not trying for this effect; he is not capable of rubato, and his playing remains merely approximate. I know I am not listening to Rubinstein here, but to an amateur who, far from being concerned about perfection or interpretation, slips into the notes he finds on the score. He sight-reads, advances a bit, and, little by little, he is led into a twilight world. Sight-reading is not merely a way to discover or learn a piece of music. It is also a naive approach to music itself. It provides easy access to the music, unburdened by a respect for the notes or by some virtuoso execution. Amateurs who sight-read feel their way about, attempting more or less to hold a line of notes while respecting a few chords. They vagabond, caring little for technical difficulties.

Sartre was a sight reader—a fact that will not surprise us. As readers, we are accustomed to the insatiable curiosity of this enthusiastic thinker who strove to cover all fields of human endeavor. Throughout his life, Sartre never stopped sight-reading the philosophy of Heidegger or Marx, the poetry of Mallarmé or Senghor, the paintings of Tintoretto, the sculptures of Giacometti, and so on. Nevertheless, sight-reading a score implies another kind of relation altogether; it conducts us ultimately toward a less triumphant exploration. One must "follow" the notes rather than decode them or attempt to uncover their hidden meaning. Hence the distinction in French between sight-reading [*déchiffrage*] and deciphering [*déchiffrement*]. Still, beyond this distinction, we should be concerned with separating the former from its usual slavish and laborious meaning. Sight-reading should not be reduced to the kind of reading typical of students starting a foreign language. Rather, it presupposes a certain way of relating to music, implying even a certain liberty, improvisation, and invention. The sight reader is a special kind of player. His way of reading music predisposes him to accompany others—singers or other instrumentalists. As a professional, she is rarely a soloist; as an amateur, alone and with no particular agenda, she goes through scores she finds at random while flipping through albums. If we keep to the original meaning of the French word, *déchiffreur*, we might believe that everything opposes the sight reader and the improviser: the latter trusts himself to his inspiration; the former is a slave to the score. Still, improvisation is a practiced art. Sometimes it is restricted to conventional developments of a given theme. As a sight reader, Sartre never intended to play for the public. He delighted instead in finding new pieces within a familiar repertory. He enjoyed going through scores as the occasion permitted, setting about to play like an actor imbibing imaginary worlds of sound.

The whole of one's being reveals itself in the body's position at the piano. In the filmed scene, Sartre is seated not on a stool or proper piano bench, but in an ordinary chair. He has not succumbed to that obsession with furniture so solicited by this instrument, the pride of bourgeois interiors. He thus sits too low, with his wrists below the keys. This position serves to emphasize his fingers, which are short and not so nimble. Experienced pianists, especially toward the end of their lives, sometimes hold their fingers a little straight, as though they no longer needed to bend them. The lack of articulation in Sartre's fingers comes rather from his being self-taught: He goes for the easiest way to hold his fingers and hits the mark. Although there is nothing terribly exceptional in such stiffness, the touch of the keys that it produces is. Sartre's fingers do not really go into the keys, but rather brush over them. Is this the hand of the philosopher that moves across the keyboard? Or a different hand, one more in line with his entire body, more fully receptive to his skin, his nerves, and his moods? The hand has been a frequent object of philosophical discourse ever since Aristotle. Sartre too, in *Being and Nothingness* [*L'être et le néant*], had produced his own thesis on this grasping and graspable appendage. He used it to take up the question of dualism: What does it mean to have a body? Am I in my body like a pilot in his ship? Using the example of his hand, Sartre answered Descartes' challenge by showing that I "am" my body. I can use my hand to write, just as I would a pen, but I cannot get rid of it, as I could a pen. We may now suggest to Sartre the example of the piano: Is the hand the same kind of instrument as the keys, or the hammers that strike chords? Is it governed by the mind, which reads and interprets the music? Or instead, is the pianist also his hand? We affirm that, yes, the pianist is his hand, and even that he is entirely in his hand. The hand most assuredly gets the whole of our consciousness involved in the world, revealing either its willingness or reticence to touch and enter into things. A handshake is sticky not because its skin is sweaty, but because it carries with it the very viscosity of the world. Sartrean characters don't care much for oily hands, which seem to exist between two states of matter—half solid, half liquid. At times, they prefer to stick a knife into their palm rather than feel it sweat through the pocket of their pants.

How then should one touch the piano keyboard? Does the warm hand that touches it leave a bit of its glistening sweat behind? Or has that hand become rigid with cold, separate from the warmth of the body? Sartre's fingers caress the keys but do not penetrate the keyboard. The ivory keys go down, of course, but the dominant movement is lateral. The hands are placed on them delicately, as if they acted upon the keys through mere contact. Sartre's touch oscillates between refinement and clumsiness. His lumbering and puffy fingers nevertheless move with tact and grace. It is often said that a bad pianist reminds us that the piano is made up of hammers. But the hands of Sartre neither strike nor hammer the keys. In their touch, they respect the smooth whiteness of the keyboard. They solicit it with a learned subtlety: Do not press the keys, do not penetrate them, but caress them instead. Sartre delighted in these same subdued connections when lovers' bodies came together. Flesh becomes a pure relation to the other, escaping from any ravenous melding of bodies. In the language of philosophy, he was discovering in this relation a "reciprocal incarnation." The hands that caress the body of another make that body exist as flesh, and, through a tactile chiasm, these guiding hands are in turn incarnated by the body they touch. They feel themselves as flesh that feels thanks to the very skin they glide across. Phenomenologists have thus, on occasion, given themselves over to erotic descriptions of the caress—though still prudish in comparison to the libertine philosophers of the eighteenth century, who were themselves quite prolix about the use of their hands. Sartre, however, more than Merleau-Ponty or Levinas, left his own attractions and repulsions open for exploration. Although the closing pages of *Being and Nothingness* on the obscenity of the feminine hole are not often the subject of university exams, they nevertheless reveal a lived truth under the surface of abstraction. The jelly that remained stuck to the mind's finger in *Being and Nothingness*, or the pebbly mud that had made Roquentin's hand sticky in *Nausea*, speak to a Sartrean repugnance at feeling one's own body plunge into a suspect substance. More a masturbator of women than a penetrating Hussar, Sartre himself caressed both beings and things, staying at their surface.

Sartre's hands on the keyboard stand out all the more because his body seems stiff. His only suppleness comes from the touch of the keys at the tips of his fingers. There is no release in his chest, which remains straight, as is often the case for short people who keep their chin up. He looks serious. We might think that this famous man, knowing he is being filmed, is putting on a bit of farce for us. But no, Sartre knows all too well these role-playing games that he has performed ever since his childhood. He caresses the keys and allows the music of Chopin to come forth. Curiously, he plays without rhythm. He follows the notes in a linear continuity that flattens out the meter. I'll come back to this oddity of his playing in a bit, since, at first "listen," it reveals Sartre's concern to remain within the unfolding of the piece and to not fall behind when confronted by some pianistic difficulty. This particular piece does not demand advanced technique, and Sartre is attempting to maintain an imagined empathy through sound. The Nocturne in G minor is, in fact, marked by melancholy. It is composed of small paintings that together reveal a mental landscape. It evinces feelings. Softly ruffling the nerves, it allows a passivity—both happy and painful—to set in. This kind of music takes control of bodies and of space in its interior plenitude. Jean-Paul and, standing behind him, Arlette fixate upon the score. They can be seen consenting to and yet shying away from the intrusive eye of the camera. Their romantic affection for each other is present in the scene, as though in the form of a quotation: Arlette and Jean-Paul love Chopin; they love each other, all the while playing Chopin.

Although he was a solitary amateur, Sartre associated music with feminine company. He played the piano at his daughter Arlette's place, just as he had played at his mother's after the war, and just as he had played at his grandmother's when he was even younger, upon returning home from school. He did not himself own an instrument in the apartment he rented, maintaining his definitive estrangement from all ownership. Playing thus meant going to someone else's place, and in particular, to a woman's place. At his mother's, on the rue Bonaparte, Jean-Paul sat himself down, in her company, on a small bench of gilded mesh in front of the piano every day between three and five in the afternoon. After that, he went back to his work, which was his writing. He later had to leave his life in the Saint-Germain-des-Prés neighborhood after militants of the *Algérie française* movement twice bombed where he was staying. In Montparnasse, he then re-created a sort of emotional geography for himself: Anne-Marie Mancy, his mother, moved to the boulevard Raspail, just as he did; Simone de Beauvoir lived on the rue Schoelcher; Arlette Elkaïm, the rue Delambre; Michelle Vian, boulevard Montparnasse. Wanda Kosakiewicz remained on the rue du Dragon. From his balcony on the tenth floor, the tribal chief could thus point out where these women lived. Sartre had on many occasions declared his preference for feminine company. He found that it suspended the power relations that often alienate the male psyche. There were certain activities one could do with women, far from the attitude of seriousness that such a nonconformist philosopher had to flee: talking about landscapes, revealing one's emotions, spending time people-watching, and so on. We might suspect de Beauvoir's companion of a bit of chauvinism here, for he seems to relegate the feminine to prattle and superficiality. But this would be to forget that Sartre felt himself to be feminine. Besides the language of authority or biting militant rhetoric (which he leveled to the point of paroxysm during the Algerian war), Sartre also sought a language free of any power drive.

How was Sartre thus able to divide up his time and his language? How was he able to be a ferocious righter of wrongs, on the one hand, and an insouciant vagabond, on the other? How could he denounce the crimes of the United States in Vietnam and those of the Soviets in Czechoslovakia, yet head off to Rome for long holidays in pleasant company, drinking cappuccinos on the terrace of the Hotel Nazionale? While this divide seems to be greatest during the 1960s, had it not existed since Sartre's childhood? We can see the little "Poulou" pretending to be the chevalier de Pardaillan, a young knight straight from the pages of the swashbuckling novels of Michel Zévaco, righting wrongs at the top of his lungs. But we can also find him taking refuge in the intimacy of his childhood gynaeceam, free from the masculine authoritarianism of his prematurely deceased father. Were there two Sartres? But then, one would have to distinguish a thousand other Sartres if we truly wanted to follow all the rhythms and writings of his life. It seems more fruitful to think in terms of connections than separations. And connections are precisely what is at work when playing the piano. It is a revelatory activity, closely tied to this taste for language beyond signification, to the imagination of feelings, and to the play of temporalities.

Music constitutes a domain of complicity. Without implying an elitism of some happy few, we know that it can only be shared with others who are predisposed to certain harmonies and tonic correspondences. Although the feminine companionship Sartre enjoyed so well might seem extensive, each companion did not have the same role. Women revolved around him until his very last days, but they were not interchangeable. In her "Love Letter to Jean-Paul Sartre," Françoise Sagan recounts how tired Sartre had become of serious conversations among men and of the solicitations made of him by young intellectuals who were looking for a father figure. His female friendships helped him forget Hiroshima, Stalin, militant stupidity, and so on: "Especially those women who would sometimes telephone him at midnight when we came back from dinner, or in the afternoon while we were having tea. They seemed so demanding, so possessive, so dependent on this infirm blind man who was now deprived of his profession as a writer. These women, by the very excessiveness of their demands on him, restored him to life, the life he had lived till then, as a ladies' man, womanizer and sometimes tender-hearted, sometimes comic storyteller." For Sartre, music, game playing, and imagination all belonged to the feminine universe. He listened to records with Sagan, who liked to hold his hand. But the piano was at Arlette's place, and he developed with her far more than a mere complicity among music lovers. When we learn that Sartre also confided his dreams to her, we begin to sense that the playing of music goes together with a certain way of relating to existence, to time, and to images. The legendary couple of Sartre and de Beauvoir might leave us with the image of a total and exclusive sharing between these two philosopher-writers, to the point where nothing could be hidden from the Beaver. All of Sartre's "contingent" relationships with other women were the object of reports and detailed letters to her. Each told the other about everything: They exchanged the smallest idea, corrected each other's manuscripts, traveled together, rebelled together, smoked together. But they rarely found themselves at the piano together—this despite Simone's efforts to practice. They were rarely together at the piano precisely because this type of exchange does not simply fall within a certain kind of knowledge or musical culture. Playing music is entirely different from listening to it or commenting upon it.

Music was instead for his daughter, as were his dreams. And we would risk missing out on a lot here if we did not investigate further this link between the piano and oneiric imaginary. All the more so because we find this association at work in another musical philosopher, Theodor Adorno, who meticulously recorded his dreams during his exile in the United States. Adorno would play the piano and then dream of Mahler and of his mother singing Kindertotenlieder. Upon his return to Frankfurt, chords in E flat major still resonated throughout the night, even though he dreamed of playing them on a board without any keys. Sartre's dreams appealed less to sounds and images. And yet we can ask: What exactly do we know of them? Stories of dreams are just that—stories, reconstructions more or less put together by a conscious subject. And Sartre was always suspicious, not only of such stories, but also of dreams themselves. He associated dreams with *mauvaise foi* (bad faith) and with a loss of consciousness—in short, with the kind of passivity that he routinely dismissed. In his work *The Imaginary* [*L'imaginaire*] he thus wrote of the dream as an activity of the mind, but he did so without disclosing his own dreams. He refused all complacency with anything that does not depend upon the self. Instead, he valued the mastery of whatever concerns our will. Faithful to Cartesian generosity, Sartre did not give any credit to dreams or to uncontrolled dreaming. And yet. . . . And yet once again, we see his discourse and his practice diverge. Sartre never ceased to question the nature of the imagination. At the age of twenty-two he devoted the work of his advanced degree to it, and he maintained a passionate interest in psychological studies on the imagination and on the ecstasies of mystics. With the help of his friend Daniel Lagache, he even experimented with mescaline in order to study hallucinatory phenomena from within. This ambition to be both experimenter and test subject allows us to take stock of Sartre's frenzy for mastery. And although the cause of philosophy may thereby have gained some brilliant pages on the imagining mind, the experimenter himself suffered from depression over the next six months as a result.

As man of control, Sartre loathed hallucinations and dreams: They were types of passive phenomena that produce metamorphoses and rearrange memories unbeknownst to the dreamer, whether awake or not. Sartre did not write down his dreams, but rather confided them orally. Unlike Adorno, he did not leave any trace of them. Nevertheless, he gave them some importance outside of his philosophical work. For Sartre at least, the activity of dreaming itself was more important than the content of dreams. No story, no image could ever capture them. They are imaginings without images. Stories can give way to secrets and shifting language, lending themselves to a continuation of their own movement. Dreams resist summary not because they seem indecent to their author, but because their mobility cannot be reduced to any symbolization. Like the playing of music, dreams were not the subject of Sartre's writing. And this does not at all diminish their importance, as indicated by both their continued role in his life and his intimate, private reminiscence of them.

This close relation between playing music and recounting dreams is not fortuitous. When Sartre plays the piano, his imagination is at work, mobilizing the history of his feelings, as well as his memories, be they dreamt or recomposed. There is some play in this musical practice, as much in terms of theater as in terms of movement. Sartre projects himself into a piece of music as though he were projecting himself onto a small theater stage. The score offers him a role: He is Chopin. He allows himself to be directed by the musical phrases, all the while trying to connect them to his own body and emotions. This time spent in music engages his imagination in that music, and he is released from the social and political realities that would otherwise engage him so completely.

The moment during which he plays is not governed by the future, by his projects or his will. Rather, while playing, he calls upon the past, allowing a strange eternity to flow forth. It undulates like a duration that will not unfold in a straight line even though it is held together by the succession of measures. The Sartrean imagination for music was linked to nostalgia, just like Adorno's dreams. But unlike Adorno, for whom music remained above all an activity that favors theory and invention, Sartre perhaps linked music to nostalgia exclusively. For while Sartre never ceased to critique familial empathy for its actual alienation, scuttling indeed any filial mythology, this same familial empathy was nevertheless maintained through the piano: Sartre would forever associate this instrument with his mother. And here we must extricate the mother from the full weight of the family. We should instead follow Barthes, who, when he was evoking his own mother, insisted on specifying *family* without *familialism*, so that the symbolic figure of the Mother would not overwhelm their loving relationship. Throughout his writings, Sartre scattered affectionate allusions to the time he spent in his childhood at the piano, thereby preventing any such psychoanalytic reductions. Let us now go back far earlier in Sartre's life to understand both his tastes and activities at the piano: for when he plays Chopin with Arlette, Anne-Marie, his mother, is not far off.

Sartre's childhood was peopled by music-loving relatives, and yet each of them played a distinct role and represented a unique relationship to music. Charles Schweitzer, his grandfather, took charge of his education after the death of his father, only a year after the boy's birth. In *The Words*, Sartre drew a portrait of his grandparents as protective guardians, guiding the literary vocation of the young genius. A professor of German, Charles transmitted a full humanist culture to Sartre and put him on the road to writing. But we should not presume that the great classical authors he thus encountered eclipsed the composers this Protestant family listened to—especially when we remember that his first cousin once removed, Albert Schweitzer, wrote a monograph on Johann Sebastian Bach. This famous minister and future Nobel Prize laureate (who, unlike Sartre, accepted the prize), was not just the "Doctor from Lambaréné"; he had earlier written a thesis on Kant and would give organ concerts for the family—assisted by the young Jean-Paul. Charles Schweitzer, moreover, was himself not without musical ambitions. And so not to be outdone, he would attempt to compose some pieces of his own while visiting his brother Louis Théophile, fellow pastor and father of Albert. Since he played in the style of Felix Mendelssohn, we might imagine that Charles used this composer to update a few pieces by Bach. For the young Sartre, music was thus associated with a religious and social activity: going to a concert, listening to music at home, being filled with spirituality, admiring the Schweitzer men, and so on. In short, it became associated with everything he would later spew back in his rejection of humanist and bourgeois models in order to assert his independence. Music's association with the Sunday service, the church organ, the Lutheran hymns, and resonating toccatas— all could have made Sartre break away from it for good. He once sarcastically observed that "faith predisposes one to musical ecstasy." We can glimpse here Sartre's hatred for concerts, which he would forever assimilate to a high mass for prominent sophisticates. There would be no ecstasy for the music-loving Sartre: He preferred a private and emotional playing.

Sartre found the antidote for church music with his mother, Anne-Marie. She would play the piano in the afternoon when his grandfather went out to give German language classes. A system of oppositions and a subterranean form of resistance thereby insidiously put itself in place: the piano against the organ, femininity against masculine authority, the imaginary against the symbolic, Chopin against Bach, fantasy against power. These divisions were never, of course, so clear-cut. For example, Sartre continued to play the works of Bach—and did so for a long time. Nevertheless, playing the piano would always be something he did in counterpoint to and away from the high politics of the world of men. Although Anne-Marie was his mother, she was also in the position of a woman-child under the guardianship of Karlémami (the collective name Sartre gave to his grandparents). She was thus like his sister and a friend with whom he shared his tastes and feelings. What music did she play when the Schweitzers were away? The ballades of Chopin, a sonata by Schumann, or perhaps Franck's variations. The young Poulou discovered a different world of music, so removed from those stiff and solemn Sundays. He would dance while his mother played, releasing his body from the Puritan weight of the Schweitzers. He would fill himself with rhythm, creating unbridled choreographies. He entered into a joyful trance, merging with the music, guided by his mother's fingers. Here at last we see the child at play: an actor without seriousness, inventing sainetes, swept away by the tempo. Exaltation replaces religious ecstasy. Sartre's taste for operettas, which might surprise more sophisticated music lovers, no doubt grew out of these moments as well. Music, love, and drama—each can be played or overplayed as a way to make fun of facile feelings or to truly live them through the work of the imagination. The mischievous young Poulou was thereby able to parody all the possible roles he could play with his mother-child. "The piano forced its rhythm on me like a voodoo drum. The Fantasia Impromptu substituted for my soul; it inhabited me, gave me an unknown past, a blazing and mortal future. I was possessed, the demon had seized me and was shaking me like a plum tree. To horse! I was mare and rider, bestrider and bestridden. I dashed over hill and dale, from the door to the window." Such musical theater, improvised with the help of Chopin, gave them a chance to escape from the austerity of their household. Jean-Paul and Anne-Marie loved each other innocently, without consequence. "But my mother has turned the page; the allegro gives way to a tender adagio; I finish off the carnage in quick time. I smile at the lady. She loves me; the music says so." Sometimes they went out to have fun together, allowing Sartre to discover another place where music and images commingled: the cinema. Anne-Marie took him to these places despite their reputation as sites of impious simulacra. At the movie theater, music was not danced to but instead accompanied a silent film. Sartre was soon seduced by these moving images, and, well in advance of other intellectuals, he recognized this as the major art form of modernity. One of his first philosophical texts was, in fact, an apology for the cinema; later, he even tried his own hand at writing screenplays and directing. Although he never spoke about the role of the piano in those childhood movie theaters, we can suppose that he found it to be an instrument decidedly disposed to such playful uses. Most of all, his experiences at the movies would have confirmed for him the intimate relationship between music and the imagination.

Playing the piano as an escape from reality took a more acute turn for Sartre when his family was recomposed by the remarriage of Anne-Marie. In the Schweitzer apartment on the rue Le Goff, the young Poulou had twirled about the piano, cutting perilous postures at the side of his mother. But he did not learn piano technique until later, during his exile (which is what he thought of it) from Paris. The circumstances of this exile are not without significance. Once again, we can see the place the piano held in Sartre's life, and the meaning that playing music had for him would be reaffirmed by this experience. Joseph Mancy, Anne-Marie's new husband, was an engineer, just like her previous husband, and indeed like Anne-Marie's brother—they were, in fact, all from the same class of the *Ecole polytechnique*. When Mancy was named head of naval constructions at La Rochelle, Sartre, aged twelve, was made to leave the lycée Henri-IV for a school outside of Paris. There he became a whipping boy for the students who could not stand the young, pretentious Parisian. While the Great War occupied the lives of the adults, he lived through the worst years of his life. This painful period would come to determine the direction of his writing. Under the watchful eye of Charles Schweitzer, Sartre had set himself out to be a writer. But it was now against the person of Joseph Mancy that he decided to write: "So he was perpetually the person I wrote against. All my life. The fact of writing was against him." Even if the piano was not consciously invested with this same mission, it nevertheless participated in the same confrontation. The Schweitzers loved the music of Bach; to play Chopin was a diversion. But Joseph Mancy did not like music, and so piano playing itself became an act of opposition.

Sartre's stepfather symbolized what he hated: science, morality, power. Music was a way to resist these three pillars of bourgeois humanism—pillars he would later find again in Flaubert's father, the doctor from Rouen. A minimal complicity was maintained between Jean-Paul and Anne-Marie: He put his fingers into hers during his musical training. At first just one, and then, little by little, his whole hand, and finally both hands in order to play together with four hands. This was how they loved each other, in the space of the keys of those seven octaves—a space over which his mother's usurper had no control. Jean-Paul played the same repertory as Anne-Marie, and he discovered orchestral music thanks to transcriptions for the piano of the symphonies of Frank or of Mendelssohn. But whereas Charles had so esteemed Mendelssohn as a composer, Jean-Paul parodied him, mixing his pieces with arias from operettas. The family comedy thus unfolded along this pianistic register. Piano playing would always remain for Sartre an at once active and passive detour through the feminine and the imagination. It would serve this purpose all the way through to 1972, when blindness ultimately kept him from playing music, just as it kept him from writing.

Sartre's relation to playing music was constructed at the very center of the familial complexes of his childhood. We would nevertheless miss its full meaning were we to limit it exclusively to maternal bonding. Childhood is not just a time of first experiences, nor is it simply a time of origin. Rather, it defines a malleable temporality that links past to present in a noncausal way. Nietzsche, who valued childhood beyond any mere nostalgia for a time gone by, described it thus: Youth arrives after adulthood, after the burden of things has been forgotten. Once one has accepted one's fate, once one's own power has been asserted, the time for play arrives; it is a time for masques and innocent joy. The young Sartre discovered music by constructing an opposition to his guardian figures. But this resistance is not reducible to some foundational structure or traumatic memory. Instead, through this opposition, he experienced a unique connection between himself as a subject and the real, as well as between himself and his own temporality. The subject who loves, perceives, and thinks, constructs itself through rhythms that are at once followed, decided upon, and combined. The hypothesis of this book is that playing music offers a privileged time for such subjectification, a time during which the ordering and disordering of a subject's relation to the real are at work.

The meaning of this playing can be found in the rhythms and arrhythmias of the person who plays in order to escape, or perhaps to parody something, or to make an affirmation. It is found in the rhythms and arrhythmias of one who plays and who, in playing, dreams, has fun, or dances. During his childhood around the maternal piano, Sartre discovered all these possibilities. Although this interpretation was contradicted by Mme Mancy herself during an interview in 1967—she was then eighty-five years old and would die two years later. She objected to her son's memories in general. She insisted on rehabilitating the memory of her father, Charles, and her husband, Joseph, declaring that Poulou didn't understand anything about his childhood. For the time being, she was worried about her son's health; she found him too thin. She also worried about Simone, whom she would like to see be more healthy ["*confortable*"]. Perhaps these last worries were not entirely unjustified. But what Mme Mancy did not understand was that this was a problem of rhythms—a problem with those very rhythms Sartre used to connect to History and to writing, as well as to music. Intellectual inspiration too is an affair of breathing and cardiac rhythm. A few years earlier, Sartre had overdosed on corydrane in order to finish writing his *Critique of Dialectical Reason* [*Critique de la raison dialectique*] as quickly as possible. This was to be his philosophical summa, integrating the results of Marxism and phenomenological analysis. What had been missing from existentialism would henceforth be recast: History, politics, economics, and society. It would reconcile Marxist philosophy with liberty, social determinism with the notion of an event, and collective history with the individual. Such ambitions required a marathon undertaking. The culmination of a theoretical revolution, this enormous book is an almost infinite jumble of a text. And, like most of Sartre's philosophical works, it leaves itself open to a next volume. The *Critique* marks the second side to Sartre's thinking, following the turning point that he himself dated to World War II. His experience of the general mobilization and of captivity at the start of the war cut his life in two: Before the war, he had set about developing an ontology of free consciousness [*la conscience libre*]; after the war, he devoted himself to the praxis of groups. Overflowing with theoretical ideas, Sartre wanted to develop a dialogue with Marxism, whatever the cost—all the more so after breaking with official communisms upon the invasion of Budapest by the Soviet Army in 1956. His abuse of corydrane in high doses, however, would damage his arterial system and cardiac rhythm for a long time to come. But such was the price to be paid for being able to write *in time*.

The *Critique* required some posthumous reorganization, but looking closely at its writing, one is struck by a certain question of rhythm. The strangeness of the work comes less from the unbelievable length of its paragraphs, or from its overall massiveness, than from the interminable sentences that link and embed multiple developments. A given sentence's subject (often difficult to identify) is overwhelmed by grammatical complements and subordinations, without any Proustian arrangement of encased subordinations. The work's reasoning unfolds freely. To follow it we would need a certain empathy with the very energy of the thinking behind it, for that thinking sets off without any rhetorical order or presupposed development. This kind of writing becomes one with its thinking—or rather, such writing follows along with its thinking. And so this jumbled book cannot be said to have been rushed by the philosopher's concern to finish it quickly, as the official version would have it. Rather, it is driven by a superhuman effort to render its writing as rapid as the movement of its thinking. Consequently, there is less a question here of rhythm than of pace. Such a phenomenon goes beyond questions of style, except insofar as we might consider style to be thought and life themselves. When writing *The Words*, Sartre had adopted the beautiful rhetoric of French classical prose; but he did so in order to take his leave from literature. He knew the score and, in turn, could compose anew. In this he was like Mendelssohn, who had taken up old forms of music (Bach and Mozart) and yet opened himself up to Romanticism. Parody is a function of composition that allows one to combine a love for language with a farewell to literature.

On the other hand, with the philosophical writing of the *Critique*, Sartre found himself in the flow of things and could never stop. He could not stop precisely because he was governed by thought, and thought itself would not stop. The slightly crazy ambition of Sartre the philosopher—an ambition equal to his earlier desire to understand hallucination through the use of mescaline—was to reduce to a minimum, which is to say completely, the separation between the flowing time of thought and the time of writing. We must understand this time of writing in the concrete sense of the term: the time it takes the pen to move across the page. The worry about a difference of times between thought and the writing of ideas is as old as philosophy itself, going back at least to Plato. But with Sartre, this worry reaches paroxysmal expression. Whatever our judgment might be about his results, we must admit that few thinkers have written so much or sought so urgently, beneath language and style, the very flow of thought. This attempt at synchrony also implies a politics of writing and links up with the Sartrean ideal of direct democracy. According to Sartre, mediations always entail a return to inertia and alienation. Movement gets clotted by parliaments, political parties, and delegations. Sartre's guiding horizon instead is to be synchronous with thought, with the event, with the collective will. Politically, he became the intellectual in synchronicity with the life of the world, engaging himself on all political fronts. Circumstantial errors were of little importance: Truths change; they too are in the process of becoming. Better to participate in the flux than to remain a complicit spectator. Never stop. Represent. Allow the time of history to flow through you. Synchronize!

In this life that is fluid and permeable to the flow of things, music is a syncopation. It does not arise as an event that interrupts some duration. Nor does it make History turn, like those events so cherished by philosophers of the rupture. Music inscribes instead a different time into the general score. This temporality can best be seen in those unique rhythms that are grafted on to the dominant flow, often keeping that flow at a distance. During the years of his greatest interventionism, Sartre maintained an almost daily routine of playing the piano. The film clip that shows him in 1967 playing a nocturne by Chopin seems unreal if we think about his intense public activity during those final years of the 1960s. He presided over the commission of inquiry of the Russell Tribunal about the crimes of the United States in Vietnam; he traveled to Egypt and Israel in order to facilitate Arab–Israeli dialogue; he supported the student movement of 1968; and he became a major figure for leftism during the 1970s. Nothing, however—neither the demonstrations, nor the meetings, nor his feverish writing—would keep him from these moments at the piano. Only blindness ended them. Far more, no doubt, than any wisdom of a philosopher removed from the world, this discrepancy among the different rhythms of a life presupposes an art of joining, a propensity to multiply oneself, and an exceptional openness to feeling.

Nevertheless the combination of diverse temporalities can also provoke interruptive syncopations. These can take the form of incompatibility or resistance, like the contretemps of a person who misses an encounter. Sartre, to be sure, having become the symbol of the engaged intellectual, did not keep all his dates. By not giving into every militant summoning from his leftist friends, he preserved for himself moments of a longer temporality. But this is not some partitioning of public and private activities. Rather, it is a negotiation between the time of the now and the times of the imagination, of writing, and of feeling. And when the Maoists pressed him to write novels for the people, instead of philosophy readable only by the bourgeoisie, Sartre resisted. He was certainly aware of the failure of socialist realism and of any subservience of writing to a political pedagogy. Above all he was "engaged" elsewhere, in the writing of his book on Flaubert. He had to explain himself on many occasions, arguing that the undertaking had political dimension: By understanding this novelist of the nineteenth century we would also come to understand the Second Empire and the general relation of writers to History. Sartre was not, therefore, deserting the Cause by studying this reactionary writer. If Sartre had tried to justify his routine playing of Chopin—a bourgeois composer forbidden in China—he would not have escaped the revolutionary tribunal! The project on Flaubert did not, of course, have the same meaning for Sartre as did his playing of Chopin. Since childhood, he had been fascinated by *Madame Bovary*. His antipathy for the author paradoxically led him to conceive a monumental study—something between a novel and a work of historical anthropology—that resulted in the three thousand pages of *The Family Idiot* [*L'idiot de la famille*], with a fourth volume to have followed. Even if the project's origin was as old as his playing of music, his emotional, imaginary, and intellectual investment in it was of a different nature, precisely because it oriented the time of Sartre's life, giving it a finality. Sartre's process of writing this book is nevertheless of great interest to us for understanding what was at play in Sartre's temporality at the moment he was writing it.

To be of one's time and to reserve time for oneself, indeed to make time—that was Sartre's challenge during these years of political activism. He supported the proletarian left; he wrote for *La cause du peuple*; he founded the newspaper *Libération*. But then, all of a sudden, Comrade Sartre excused himself: Apologies, he has an appointment with Flaubert. What kinds of philosophical questions does he treat in this work? It is, to be sure, about time: about the psychological, linguistic, and historical incarnation of a unique individual who swallowed and digested his own time in the writing of *Madame Bovary*. Sartre combined all possible approaches in order to understand this man in his time, seeking a synthesis of all types of knowledge, which he labeled the "progressive-regressive" method. This method entails a movement back and forth from the individual to history. It sought not to fix the individual person as an object of study, but to find the movement through which that person gave meaning to his past determinations by projecting them toward the future. But Sartre also investigated a time different from the one that had historically programmed Flaubert. He analyzed the mismatches, the misunderstandings that arise in the relation of an individual to his own time; which is to say, he analyzed Flaubert's anachronisms. Sartre's text thereby constructs a mirroring reflection for himself, as though he were addressing his own relation to political and historical time.

On the surface, Sartre's argument keeps to its philosophical and polemic heading: He critiques "scientific" Marxism and its determinist and reductive notion that writers merely reflect their social conditionings. A book and its author blur and deviate from the representation they are supposed to give of their class and their time. They are instead shot through with numerous temporalities. In particular, they contain that temporality in which different generations come together at a given time. Although individuals may share the same present, each may have very different durations and rhythms. The contemporaneousness of an author and his public implies achronism, for an author may be ahead of his readers.

According to Sartre, Flaubert had thus, prior to writing *Madame Bovary*, already made himself for the Second Empire, even before that political entity was foreseeable. We must distinguish here synchronicity—a synthetic cut that allows one to grasp a condensation of time in a precise moment—from diachronicity—which corresponds to the living time of becoming, with its curves and variations that are graphed along the general axis of duration. What was Sartre saying about himself through his argument? He was not a symbol of his times, even if he wanted the movement of history to flow through him. He never came to know how to completely identify himself with a collective cause, even if that cause were the truth of history on the march. Instead, he always created negotiations, misunderstandings, comings and goings among the tangled temporalities of an individual. Yet, for all that, Sartre attempted to think through a joining of temporalities, for he still believed in History and its all-encompassing movement. He therefore deliberately formulated the idea of "solutions of continuity" [*solutions de continuité*] to refer to the unique ways an individual creates to arrange his time into the historical continuum. Human time is thus constituted by multiple "profiles of temporalization." Through the deviation and inflation of an individual's own plan for existence, these profiles of temporalization give human time the shape of a spiral. During his life, Sartre maintained individual meetings not just with Flaubert and Chopin, but also with so many other people, places, and feelings, which would be impossible to name. These meetings participated in the curvature of his own existence and helped create "solutions of continuity."

Always skillfully handling the discourse of mastery, Sartre hoped to give reason itself the orientations and reversals that had defined his own existence. He created for himself a representation of all these times, in both diachronicity and synchronicity.

He never stopped going back to his own intellectual, literary, and philosophical trajectory in order to explain its philosophical, literary, and political curves, turns, and ruptures. With some regularity, Sartre would take stock of his own internal revolutions; he thereby maintained the illusion of being the author of his own time, of orchestrating his own births and rebirths. This fantasy of autogeneration was what fascinated him about revolutionary movements, and it seized him in the representation of his own internal time. His reader is not obligated to give in to this same fantasy, despite the tendency of biographers and commentators to try to smooth over any fractures [*solutions de continuité*]. Monographs map out a linear path and categorize salient traits into periods. Everything is arranged so as to edify the "man of the century." But behind every evidence of a synchronous relation between an author and his time, we also find unique rhythms, anachronies, idiorhythms, and untimeliness—we encounter a fluid, diffracted, and subterranean time. Playing the piano is part of these discrete temporalities, which escape any discourse of mastery and are subject to the risks of passivity and discontinuity.

Can we imagine a different Sartre—as a pianist who gives recitals? No doubt such an image seems out of place; it fails to correspond to the one we have of the philosopher climbing atop a barrel at Billancourt to exhort the workers who stood behind their factory gate. Yet we can indeed catch Sartre dreaming of just that, of being a professional pianist. He imagined an entirely different life for himself, one devoted to playing and composing. Curiously, despite the musical repertory he had played since childhood, Sartre did not see himself as a classical concert pianist. No, instead he would rather swap his career as a writer–philosopher to be a jazz pianist. We might be even more surprised by this secret ambition when we realize that Sartre did not play jazz! Perhaps this was due to a certain difficulty of rhythm encountered in jazz, which is so difficult for classical players to grasp. Sight-reading a score does not suffice. In order to play this type of music, you have to attain something like swing, which exceeds its notes while remaining indispensable to them. No doubt Sartre's dream of being a jazz pianist cannot be fully explained by musical taste. It implies a *habitus*, an imagination, and a life—a life this reject from the austere Schweitzer family would have loved to have had access to. We find the imagery of jazz at the end of *Nausea* when Roquentin begins compulsively listening to the jazz tune "Some of These Days." This song is supposed to sublimate all the disenchantment experienced by this central character, who is bogged down in a world emptied of meaning.

Nevertheless the representation that Sartre gives to jazz in this work from 1938 is contradictory and complex. In it he mixes the search for a pure essence of music with the supposed impurity of jazz. Here the piano cedes its place to an instrument more characteristic of jazz, the saxophone. In this song the saxophone gives off the sound Sartre wishes to magnify. "To drive existence out of me, to rid passing moments of their fat, to twist them, dry them, purify myself, harden myself, to give back at last the sharp, precise sound of a saxophone note." This desire for pure music is the last metamorphosis of Roquentin. It offers an end to those meanders in which Sartre had diluted pure consciousness: oily skin, sweaty touches, and unsettled weather are all now put into relief by the charm of a piece of jazz music that provides not only the tone but also the model for a redeemed existence—justified at last. To transform one's body into an instrument and to live like a melody—this would be the possible exit from contingency, a way to keep the self from being compromised among things. Disgust and anxiety suddenly seem resorbed in the purification of substances; breathing becomes easier. Only music remains. It is self-justified, not requiring extrinsic reasons. It is pure essence, without residue or excess, appropriate and adequate for what it does and what it is. The four notes of this final melody, "Some of These Days," belong to a higher realm, a realm beyond the voice, sounds, vibrations, or the crackling of a wax disc. The conclusion to this journal of a bleak life is constructed as a final resolution of all themes, proposing music as infinite closure, a fermata to human facticity, which is suddenly subsumed by the experience of sonorous purity.

But should we take this ideal of music seriously? Does it relate to jazz? And does it come to define the relationship between Sartre and music? The idea that there is a purity to art that music alone can attain has been circulating since the end of the nineteenth century. Sartre, without adhering to this idea, nevertheless strangely takes it up for this one jazz song. Following the inspiration from Flaubert for a "book about nothing," modernists promoted the potentiality of a work to free itself from everything that it is not. Music offered these writers the paragon of a form or material completely released from the persistent meaning of words. Pure style, pure art, pure form—such principles were at the root of the claim for an autonomy of art, made by both modernists and the avant-garde. But the four "pure" notes of the saxophone seem an odd choice to illustrate this ambition. Sartre integrates them into a modernist rhetoric that goes against both the practice of jazz and his own relation to Romantic music. Pure art, removed from meaning and feeling, describes a perfect form and a perfect time, which follow only their own laws. Nothing could be farther removed from the emotional exchange of a jazz session! It is moreover revealing that the musical experience put forward by Roquentin does not take place live, but rather comes only from a recording of the music. Such supposed purity requires an exclusive relation between the music and a listener who is removed from the conditions of the music's performance. Indeed, behind the more or less parodic discussion of the narrator about pure music lies the recording. A record privileges the imagination and enables the scene of a man, alone, who can project himself into the role of the musician. And that is where, without doubt, Sartre's interior theater reveals itself: The ideal of musical purity dissolves in favor of role-playing.

The jazz composer Roquentin wishes to identify himself with is a New York Jew, whom Sartre describes as living in feverish inspiration in a Manhattan apartment some twenty stories up.

The American with the black eyebrows sighs, gasps and the sweat rolls down his cheeks. He is sitting, in shirtsleeves, in front of his piano; he has a taste of smoke in his mouth and, vaguely, a ghost of a tune in his head. "Some of These Days." Tom will come along in an hour with his hip-flask; then both of them will lower themselves into leather armchairs and drink brimming glasses of whisky and the fire of the sky will come and inflame their throats, they will feel the weight of an immense, torrid slumber. But first the tune must be written down. "Some of These Days." The moist hand seizes the pencil on the piano. "Some of these days you'll miss me, honey."

That's the way it happened. That way or another way, it makes little difference. That is how it was born. It is the worn-out body of this Jew with black eyebrows which it chose to create it. He held the pencil limply, and the drops of sweat fell from his ringed fingers on the paper. And why not I?

A tune composed by a Jew and sung by a "Negro woman with a husky voice." The purity of the saxophone is thus fractured, for it plays a music created by people who were, to the minds of racist ideologies at the end of the 1930s, inferior races only capable of producing a degenerate art, like jazz.

But Sartre has confused everything here. As the Sartre scholar and jazz critic Michel Contat has noted, this ragtime tune was composed by an African-American, Shelton Brooks, and sung by a white woman. And even the saxophone was in fact a clarinet!

The history Sartre invented for the song abounds in clichés and confirms that he dreamt up a jazz musician's life through his empathetic reading of stories from the United States—stories that he may have seen at the movies or read in the novels of Dos Passos. He did finally discover the atmosphere of a jazz club for himself when he visited New York in 1945. Nick's Bar was rather different from the College Inn he had frequented a bit in Montparnasse. It immersed him in a world where drinking and smoking continued through the night, allowing him to become fully engrossed in this lively music. Sartre came to forget about listening to jazz on records, offering his famous phrase: "Jazz is like bananas: it has to be eaten on the spot." When a bit more inspiration came to him, he defined jazz as "the music of the future," reappropriating that old description of Wagner's music. (He had earlier said as much about the cinema.) Back in Paris, he got to meet Charlie Parker and Miles Davis through Michelle and Boris Vian. For Sartre the jazz musician had a unique status: He is neither performer nor composer; instead, he is his instrument and his work. As he said in reference to John Coltrane: "He arrives, he is named so-and-so, he plays his instrument. The name of the musician is part of the work of jazz." The jazzman is more than a style of music, more than pieces of music. He incarnates a life that Sartre himself would have loved to know, or at least one that Sartre loved to imagine himself living.

Was Sartre, then, a jazzman manqué? For someone who regularly played Chopin, jazz no doubt came closer to imagination than to music. But even after updating his repertory, Sartre stayed within a classical register. He appreciated Schoenberg more than rock or pop, which left him cold. Although he appreciated ad lib compositions and live improvisations, he only tried them himself on Romantic harmonies. In private, Sartre improvised in the style of Chopin or Webern; he even allowed Arlette to record him. Without any pretensions to innovation, he nevertheless conveyed his own *feeling*. Freely varying the inflexions of the melodies and chords, they transported him toward worlds without power. They thus took him out of the general linearity of time and loosened his engagement with his own times. Only rarely did he risk writing his music down; at the very most he composed a sonata in the style of Debussy. But Sartre described this as a simple, private exercise. It is noteworthy that he stuck to the sonata form instead of trying, through Debussy, to use intervals capable of disrupting traditional forms.

Neither truly a performer nor a composer, Sartre maintained a high level of control over the piano, a control that had been developed in his childhood. The most striking thing about this style of playing lies in its persistence over time and its compatibility with Sartre's other activities, to which it might otherwise appear heterogeneous. Of course we can delight in the discovery of musical tastes discordant with Sartre's extraordinary interest in whatever was new in the world of art. But ultimately his repertory is not the heart of the matter, because for the amateur, music is not confined to a particular know-how or to a particular corpus. Taste counts for less than the actual playing. Music held an indescribable place in Sartre's life; it did not pass through language because it involved feelings and time. Reading a musical score imposes certain rhythms and durations that can unhook one's relation to the immediacy of reality, and even to the necessity of reality. The scene of a record turning on the gramophone in *Nausea* presents music as a blade cutting through the dreariness of the world, setting the hardness of the needle against it. Nevertheless the amateur Sartre himself did not experience music like this. His piano playing privileged far more the fluttering and subtle movement of temporalities. Philosophy and music come together through him in a unique relation that we cannot fold into some philosophy of music, like that of Adorno. Music is an activity, a disposition of life. If there is a thinker who took music to its highest existential value, it was Nietzsche, whom we can indeed find smuggled into Sartre's work. Everything would seem to oppose the aristocratic thinker Nietzsche to the anti-elitist philosopher Sartre. We recall that Sartre even used to throw water on his Nietzschean friends, shouting: "Thus pissed Zarathoustra." And yet these two shared a similar admiration for Chopin. There are those who will object that this is a mere detail. But a great deal, if not everything, gets told through such choices. As Nietzsche maintained: All of life is a discussion of tastes and colors. Whether one prefers Pergolèse or Rameau, Beethoven or Rossini, Wagner or Bizet, Schoenberg or Stravinsky, Glenn Gould or Samson François reveals affinities of thought more profound than any conceptual opposition.

Sartre could never have been indifferent to Nietzsche, who was a good pianist, composer, and philosopher. This must have been especially true when, at the age of twenty, Sartre was hesitating between a life of literature or one of philosophy, all the while continuing to play the piano. In 1927, he sketched out a novel inspired by the stormy relationship between Nietzsche, Wagner, and Wagner's wife. As usual, the young Jean-Paul oscillated between parody and empathy in identifying with his characters. The main character of this novel, *A Defeat* [*Une défaite*], is an ambitious *normalien*, named Frédéric, who is taken with the will to power.

He admires the writer and composer Richard Organte and wishes to write a book about him. Invited over by this maestro, who is famous and narcissistic, he falls in love with his wife, Cosima, an ingénue who allows this new admirer to satisfy the needs of his imagination. Frédéric even becomes the private tutor to their children. But the great man Organte is more skillful than he is a genius. He comes to disappoint Frédéric, who believes himself to be the bearer of the philosophy of the future. Ultimately, the couple breaks off their relationship with him. We easily recognize the story here of the young Nietzsche, who was fascinated by Richard Wagner during the writing of his first great work, *The Birth of Tragedy*, and who took as his model the man he believed to be a genius. We recognize the Wagner couple's disdain for Nietzsche's music and ambitions, the ambivalence of Cosima Wagner toward Nietzsche, and then his emancipation from this couple. The events of Nietzsche's biography interested Sartre in more than one respect. Cosima Wagner was not entirely a stranger to his own family: Albert Schweizter had had the privilege of meeting her in her old age at Bayreuth. And Sartre also transposed into her the image of a mature woman whom he desired, whose son became his own pupil. Richard Wagner, aka Organte, receives a sarcastic portrait in Sartre's novel, and Sartre's anti-German tinge is so flagrant that we surmise that he was settling accounts here with the Schweitzers. The German maestro sings with exaggerated movement of his jaw, purses "his lips ferociously revealing his teeth." Suddenly inspiration is upon him: "He rushed to the piano and began singing again amidst the splashes of notes." He boasted thus: "Listen closely: *tra tra la la tra tra la la*, there was his arrogance, *la la la*, and the *same*, and then *this* and *that*, *boom boom*." We might think we are reading here some of Nietzsche's more scathing pages written after his break with Wagner in which he described such "Teutonic schlock."

Was Sartre thus showing his affinity to a Nietzschean repulsion for such music? Did he see himself in this portrait of a philosopher at the dawn of some great work? Frédéric is, after all, supposed to start writing a dramatic elegy about Empedocles, which would affirm his own genius and transform his personal defeat into victory. But Sartre himself never stopped denouncing such mystification: Imitation is not limited to childhood dreaming, or to this overlap of feelings and ambitions between two piano-playing philosophers. Sartre's closeness to Nietzsche involves foremost an imaginary contamination based on admiration and parody. Also in the mix is the complicity with the solitary man, as well as the denunciation of the young Romantic in wont of the sublime. And behind this iconoclastic play of Sartre against himself, via Frédéric, lies an even deeper ambivalent relation of the subject to his own times. Disrupting the world through transvaluation or revolution also requires a pause, an arrhythmia, a unique tempo that was, for Sartre, his piano playing.

Saint-Denis, rue de la Liberté, Spring 2007

Three

WHY I AM A GREAT PIANIST

Nietzsche's legacy can be seen in unexpected places. Sometimes we find it in a small wooden frame decorating a room in one's home, or perhaps inscribed above an entryway: "Without music, life would be a mistake." Every music lover, no matter how unfamiliar with philosophy, knows this maxim, and the importance that Nietzsche accorded to music has largely been established. Although he was not much read during his own lifetime, this philosopher wrote to his friends that monuments would be constructed to his work in a hundred years . . . or perhaps five hundred, or a thousand. Yet, whatever confidence he may have had that his texts would bring him such celebrity, his greater hope was to be known for his musical projects. A philologist and philosopher, Nietzsche was also a pianist and composer who maintained a lifelong desire for a career as a musician. The lack of success for his compositions did not discourage his reflections on music, and those who have written on his work have given music exemplary status for his entire philosophy. Was Nietzsche, then, an unlucky musician who turned to philosophy? Or rather a philosopher-musician who transformed thought into art? For is not his great work *Thus Spoke Zarathustra* a sublime symphonic poem?

Such questions go beyond Nietzsche's own life: Thanks to him, and the music-loving Schopenhauer before him, music became not only a privileged object for philosophy but also an ideal—an issue of aesthetic and metaphysical import, a touchstone for all human activities and human values. Commentators on Nietzsche have thus used his references to music as though they formed a score with many key signatures, allowing his varied and sometimes contradictory works to be read as a whole. His tumultuous relationship with Wagner revealed the principal stakes in the meaning and future of art, as well as thought. Discussions of this relationship, however, have long remained rather theoretical and text-based. But over the last few years, thanks to the publication of Nietzsche's musical works by Curt Paul Janz, readers of his texts who also know how to read music have been able to rediscover this philosopher in light of his own compositions. Even though his output was not of such quality as would be revelatory for the history of music, its very abundance merits our attention. Nietzsche's approximately seventy works—*lieder*, symphonies, choral works, various piano pieces—cannot be reduced to a mere hobby divorced from his philosophical writing. On the contrary, they lie at the very heart of his thinking, as well as the changes that occurred within that thinking. We can no longer write about the decisive role music played in his thought without now listening to his own music!

In keeping with the subject of this book, I am most interested in Nietzsche as a pianist and in the implications this instrument had on his tastes, his feelings, and his imagination. Which composers did Nietzsche play? How did he play them? When? And with whom? Nietzsche did not himself discuss this habitual activity of his. We must approach it more obliquely, through the accounts of others or through his indirect allusions to it. To approach Nietzsche through his piano playing we must first put his writings about music and his musical compositions aside. We shall come back to them later with this instrument fully in mind. But for now, we must leave them aside because, before writing about music and before composing his own pieces, Nietzsche, like any other amateur, had to learn music. He did so, of course, from a repertory within a particular style of playing, arising from the familial and social practices that surrounded him. And even after he began to create his own pieces of music, he continued, with some frequency, to play his favorite composers. Have critics found this Nietzsche to be of little interest simply because we lack the necessary revelatory documents? Or perhaps because this Nietzsche seems so at odds with the great musicological debates into which we have otherwise billeted his thought? Taking up this question of critical neglect should allow us to dislodge some entrenched oppositions.

Nietzsche began his study of the piano at about the age of nine. He was a particularly gifted student, with a passion for Bach, Handel, Haydn, and Mozart. After just two years of study he was already playing Beethoven's sonatas. The son and grandson of ministers, he was born into a world of organ music and choral singing. But when he was four, his father, whose mind had become deranged, died. When Friedrich would later dream of him, he saw his father in the church and heard organ music resonating. Once Nietzsche had left the town of his birth, he set himself to playing the piano. He did so surrounded by his mother and his sister, later dedicating his first compositions to them. Nietzsche would always associate piano playing with a shared intimacy, a union of solitude and communion. He sent his scores to his sister Elisabeth, indicating the particular interpretation that she should follow when playing. He did the same with his music-loving friends: Gustav Krug, Erwin Rohde, Franz Overbeck, Heinrich Köselitz (aka Peter Gast). He composed pieces for four hands or for two pianos, offering his playing, as well as his compositions, as a dialogue intended to map out constellations of friendships. For Nietzsche, the stakes of piano playing specifically involved playing with, in front of, or for another person. In playing, the point was to hear each other, more than to understand each other. In his abundant correspondence, Nietzsche frequently evoked the pieces that he was working on, whether his own or those of his preferred composers. He entered into dialogue with them because he felt that, thanks to music, he too belonged among these beings for whom language had been transformed into art. When he recounted those moments of intense solitude he felt while holed up in some lousy boardinghouse room during one of his many wanderings, Nietzsche would describe the pianos he rented, their ivory keys and mahogany boxes. The mere presence of this instrument created a familiar environment for him by summoning up the artists whose works he played on them. From his student days at Pforta, Bonn, and Leipzig, to his very last days along the Mediterranean at Genoa, Rome, Nice, or Torino, Nietzsche always created a place for himself where he could be with his preferred composers—which is to say his chosen family.

Most biographies of Nietzsche stop in 1889 at the onset of his madness. They end at the moment, conveniently called his breakdown, in which he threw himself around the neck of a horse that was being beaten by a coachman in Torino. Indeed there is nothing left to read or say once this philosopher had been brought back to Basel. He was moved to his mother's place, and then, finally, to his sister Elisabeth's place in Weimar. Elisabeth had since become Mrs. Förster and would later become a Nazi, arrogating Nietzsche's legacy to that cause. For those last eleven years of his life, we can only guess at his illness and speculate about his family's maneuverings over his intellectual heritage. Out of his madness and the drama surrounding it, myths and conjectures arise. Was it syphilis, a brain tumor, psychosis, or hereditary degeneration? We base our after-the-fact diagnoses on the quotations the philosopher left behind, or sometimes on quotations reported by those close to him who witnessed the progressive end of his cerebral activity. But we forget to mention that Nietzsche's incoherence at the end, or even his aphasia, did not stop him from playing the piano. After being committed to a psychiatric clinic in Jena, he still played two hours every day, performing and improvising on the upright piano in the cafeteria. Köselitz even wondered whether his friend wasn't just pretending to be mad, so brilliant was his inspired playing. Overbeck, for his part, tells of taking Nietzsche out for walks and of how he tried to converse with him despite Nietzsche's attempts to strike out at the dogs or people they passed. But Nietzsche had by then abandoned any dialogue with others through words, maintaining only the sublime language of musical notes. His mouth was silenced, and only his hands remained. Those hands had definitively swapped the blank page for the piano keyboard.

What do we know about Nietzsche's hands? Lou Salomé described them in a book she wrote about this man who had reserved his only love for her: They were incomparably beautiful and fine. Had they touched her body? The enthusiasm Nietzsche felt for this woman—who would become Rilke's muse and later incarnate for Freud that troubling femininity—was disappointed when he found that he had to share his friendship for her with Paul Rée. No doubt her sensual description of his hands was based on how they looked on the piano. And Lou Salomé, in choosing this part of Friedrich's body, wished to emphasize his elegance and physical and spiritual dexterity. She did not seek to define his hands as those of a philosopher, hands that would put ideas to paper. If such had been her intention, she would not have insisted on the feminine softness of his movements. Remaining true to Nietzsche's own thought, she attempted to approach the man through the gravitation of his body, capturing his skill for lightness and nimble shifts. In an aphorism from *Beyond Good and Evil*, Nietzsche wondered at the habit certain people have of hiding their faces in their hands in order not to show their emotions. He observed how often hands betray their owner: Their position, shape, and scars form a unique landscape.

A whole person is revealed in their hands. And who knows this better than a pianist? According to a few accounts, Nietzsche's piano playing was at once powerful and twirling. One gets the sense that he cared more about the impression conveyed than precision. At times brutal in his playing, the philosopher wished to make his instrument resonate as much as possible. One friend and confidant, Malwida von Meysenbug, at whose place in Rome Nietzsche first met Lou, recalled his sweeping and polyphonic playing. Such descriptions should best be related to the specific pieces he was playing, for while the piano is the most orchestral of all the instruments, one plays it differently for a Wagner transcription than for a Schumann melody. Nietzsche's piano training leads us to believe that he respected the role reserved for each hand. Yet this relationship was changed considerably during the time of his admiration for Wagner. His own compositions from this time palpably emphasize resonances and harmonic modulations over the entire range of the piano. Nietzsche's hands are eloquent; they have their own style that corresponds to the psyche of the philosopher-musician. Nevertheless the language they speak had been created by those who composed the music. When Nietzsche gave his own opinion on the proper role for each hand, his diagnosis was not limited to some question of technique. Rather, it involved his entire under-standing of music and of the relations of speech to the culture that maintains it. In 1881 Nietzsche wrote: "At the piano, the important thing is to let the song sing and the accompaniment accompany." His Wagnerian period was over, and now he returned to a style of play that clearly separated melody, song, and underlying harmonic. A score's indications could no longer be disregarded, nor could one play it nervously: The music must sing. Nietzsche held this concep-tion so firmly that he considered it to be an almost physiological necessity, as well as a philosophical weapon. And so we can ask: Who were the composers who imprinted this conception on him?

Most of the studies devoted to Nietzsche's musical tastes are about his love/hate for Wagner, or the antidote he found in Bizet. But Nietzsche never denied his passion for Chopin. This Roman-tic vein has been commented upon, although more often through Schumann, whose *Manfred* Nietzsche explicitly discussed. So why this lack of critical attention to Chopin, who hardly gets mentioned in the scholarly musicological reflections on Nietzsche? Simply put: This Romantic composer doesn't seem worthy of philosophical discussion; he is not serious enough, not German enough. Most of all, he is absent from the great musical debates of the age and from the artistic battles dramatized by Nietzsche. Although Cho-pin did not come to symbolize a particular aesthetic position, and although he was more listened to and performed than analyzed, this should not imply that he held any lesser importance. On the contrary. Unlike most of the composers Nietzsche passed judgment upon—sometimes favorably, sometimes unfavorably—Chopin was always praised, loved, and played by this philosopher-musician. The few mentions Nietzsche makes of Chopin's works (admittedly few) are always moments of elation and grateful recognition.

To say that Nietzsche appreciated Chopin would be too weak: He adored him; he identified with him. In his *The Wanderer and His Shadow*, Nietzsche makes Chopin the king of the arts:

> The last of the modern composers to behold and worship beauty as Leopardi did, the inimitable Pole, Chopin—no one before or after him has a claim to this epithet—Chopin possessed the same princely nobility in respect of convention as Raphael shows in the employment of the simplest, most traditional colours, however, but in regard to traditional forms of melody and rhythm. These, as *born to etiquette*, he admits without dispute, but does so playing and dancing in these fetters like the freest and most graceful of spirits—and does so, moreover, without turning them to ridicule.

Freiheit, Schönheit, Vornehmheit, der freieste und anmutigste Geist. . . . Nietzsche marshals the most laudatory concepts and qualities to convey the uniqueness, the incomparableness of that event known as Chopin. Behind these praises, he outlined an aesthetics that, in its different versions, links freedom and constraint, simplicity and elegance. In *The Birth of Tragedy* Nietzsche had linked Wagner to the spirit of ancient Greece. Here, without explicitly saying so, he again takes up an implicit understanding of the tragic: Freedom and power come about through an accepted fate. In art, creation is forged from well-understood constraints.

Chopin did not seek to break with or go beyond musical conventions; he sublimated them. He played them like a king who has left behind the solemnity of power in order to compose a few aristocratic figures. In terms of artistic creation, what distinguishes Chopin from Wagner goes to the elegant simplicity of his forms, the subtlety of his arabesques, which are far removed from any emotional or stylistic overflow. During this same period, Nietzsche confessed to finding in Chopin the highest sense of form, which is to say extremely refined developments resting on simple, elementary structures. In a note from 1878, written at the time of his break with Wagner, Nietzsche's assessment of Chopin testifies to his fidelity to this composer. Before his discovery of Bizet, he considered Chopin as an alternative to the maestro from Bayreuth. But Nietzsche's opposition to Wagner had not yet been formulated in quite this way. Rather, at that time Nietzsche was preferring to play Chopin over Schumann, whom he then considered an "old maid." But why would Nietzsche make such an attack against someone like Schumann, who had nevertheless inspired him? Herein the question of Romanticism gets sorted out, with Nietzsche reversing the values normally assigned to each of the two composers. He mocked Schumann as the incarnation of that particular young man—sickly, self-indulgent, and maudlin—which was dreamt up by the French and Germans at the beginning of the nineteenth century. And this cliché of the Romantic gets associated with Schumann, the German composer with whom Nietzsche wanted, and indeed needed, to split, however close he may have felt to him.

Recollecting his closeness to Schumann, Nietzsche wrote that his own youthful improvisations had been as dark and hopeless as possible, in the Romantic style. Still, this critical look back on his adolescent pessimism notwithstanding, Nietzsche would associate music with tears throughout his life. And when, in his letters, he described the concerts that inspired him, he regularly mentioned breaking down into tears. Emotion was thus not rejected. Instead, Nietzsche used emotion to point to a pathology at work in Romanticism, perhaps in order to cure that same temptation that was so strong in him. Schumann becomes associated with the depression and madness that will later affect Nietzsche. By rejecting him, Nietzsche was also able to settle accounts with Wagner, even though Wagner himself had never assumed any Romantic kinship with Schumann. But for Nietzsche, Wagner had taken Romanticism to the extreme: He was the most Romantic of the Romantics; he took the German spirit's tendency to nervous passion, its inclination to destabilize the self, and its bent toward the abyss of melancholy all to their ultimate degeneracy. Wagner had radicalized the Romantic taste for folklores by glorifying traditions and ancestries in an exclusively Teutonic version. Chopin embodied the flip side of Romanticism, and Nietzsche hoped to clear him—against all evidence—of any melancholic or morbid indulgences.

In the symbolic geography of Nietzsche's mind, Chopin's music belongs to Italy. It has Italy's lightness, simplicity, and elegance. Chopin's music thus falls within a paradigm Nietzsche would hammer out little by little that pitted the Germanic north against the Mediterranean south, the Romanticism of abyssal mists against the Romanticism of a dry and luminous climate. Chopin belonged to the imaginary homeland of Raphael and Leopardi, and was thus closer to Rossini or Bellini than to Schumann—even if Schumann himself had doffed his hat to Chopin, recognizing him as a genius. Sometimes Nietzsche associated Chopin with Mozart or Haydn, but still he observed that all three shared a taste for, and even the spirit of, Italian opera. They transformed sorrowful sentiments into a music that danced; just as in opera, the natural and ugly cry of passion is transformed into melodious song. Chopin's Italian inspiration seems confirmed by Nietzsche's favorite piece, the Barcarole in F-sharp major. Indeed, the origin of this musical form can be found in the swaying of Venetian boats and the songs of the gondoliers. But Nietzsche's particular choice here is not limited to this work's Italian motif. Rather, it addresses one of Chopin's major works. Like his nocturnes, this barcarole maintains its nostalgic sentiment without giving way to sentimental empathy, for it does not seek some dramatic effect. The rhythmic swaying of the left hand never gives way, but allows different modulations to develop, all the while conserving a balance that the arpeggios of the right hand freely threaten.

The Barcarole represents the Venice Chopin dreamt of. It conveys the restrained temptation found in someone who could imagine a new departure but who remained exiled in France. It was just after having given up on a trip to Italy that Chopin composed this piece while staying at the house of George Sand at Nohant, in Berry. There he was surrounded by friends who had come to stay with this welcoming writer. Chopin would sometimes perform for the group, or else retire alone to a room upstairs that Sand had set aside for him. Her house was a regular meeting place for artists and writers. Franz Liszt and Marie d'Agoult—the future parents of Cosima Wagner—often stayed there. Like Chopin and Sand, these two embodied the musician-writer couple, which Nietzsche himself would have liked to reinvent with Lou Salomé. While there, Liszt played Beethoven and Schubert and improvised at the piano with unequaled virtuosity. Chopin, who was less social and more taciturn, withdrew upstairs while the guests feasted below, leaving them to debate the great philosophical and political ideas of the day. George Sand had succeeded in re-creating at Nohant a veritable Parisian salon. Still, a great deal of seduction must have been used to attract the likes of Balzac, Delacroix, Dumas, Gautier, Flaubert, and Turgenev into the countryside where the nearest town bears the uninviting name La Châtre, which echoes of castration.

Although Nietzsche was an admirer of French literature, he did not care for George Sand, nastily characterizing her as a milking cow with a "nice style." Sand, after all, had thought Chopin a dolt on meeting him for the first time. Nietzsche obviously couldn't stand her rural, Rousseauiste side—the way she acted like an aristocrat putting on democratic airs. In his *Twilight of the Idols*, Nietzsche made his case against Sand's writing:

> I have read the first *Lettres d'un voyageur*: like everything deriving from Rousseau false, artificial, fustian, exaggerated. I cannot endure this coloured-wallpaper style; nor the vulgar ambition to possess generous feelings. The worst, to be sure, is the female coquetting with male mannerisms, with the manners of ill-bred boys. —How cold she must have been withal, this insupportable authoress! She wound herself up like a clock—and wrote . . . Cold, like Hugo, like Balzac, like all Romantics as soon as they started writing! And how complacently she liked to lie there, this prolific writing-cow, who had something German in the bad sense about her, like Rousseau her master, and who was in any case possible only with the decline of French taste!

Between the lines of this lethal attack, Nietzsche symbolically pit Italy against the camaraderie of Nohant. His preferred novelist was Stendhal who wrote for the happy few and championed those particularly Italian refinements. He symbolized the antithesis to Balzac, Hugo, or Sand. Nietzsche thereby rearranged artistic alliances and pronounced the cultural divorce of this Sand–Chopin couple at Nohant. Instead, he put Stendhal and Chopin to one side, Sand and Liszt to the other. He set them into opposition just as he pitted Italy against Germany, or perhaps Austria, which was then occupying Italy. Nietzsche further attacked Liszt as merely a "virtuoso . . . with women." His massacres nevertheless spared— and would always spare—Chopin, whom he would recuperate and save from prostrate Germanism. Nietzsche listened to Chopin's Barcarole often, for it had value to him as an artistic and cultural dissent. Especially with regards to Nohant, it signified a difference and a strangeness for which Italy was the name, the frontier, and the place of exile.

Nietzsche's musical and cultural affiliation with Italy was, of course, the product of a choice he made and a taste that he elevated to the status of a philosophical decision. Nevertheless this radicalization of the passions he championed, together with the system of opposition they established, participated in a genealogical fantasy that at times could even change the story of his own origins. The Italianization of Chopin allowed Nietzsche to bring his favorite composer into harmony with Mediterranean culture. But Chopin is more known for his Polish origins, and so Nietzsche also constructed a family romance for himself that this time would carry him to Eastern Europe. Nietzsche came to imagine that he had Polish ancestors on his father's side—the Nietzki family, who were aristocratic Protestants supposed to have left their country a century before due to religious persecutions. Nietzsche thus constructed a countergenealogy that introduced foreign blood into his family in order to contest his German side. At first glance, we might believe that this was a rather unremarkable attempt at ennoblement on the part of someone who was so concerned with distinguishing himself. But this would be to forget both that Nietzsche's aristocratism was not based on race and that the superiority of the Superman still lay ahead—here it is a horizon and not an origin. Above all, this use of genealogy by the author of *On the Genealogy of Morals* must be all the more complicated for it. In that work, which sought to dismantle the elaboration of moral concepts, Nietzsche exposed the sedimentation of values without promoting the search for an originary truth. His invention of noble Polish ancestors was not an attempt to root his superiority in distant origins. Rather, it was about blurring his German heritage by introducing a Slavic signifier. It matters little whether Nietzsche believed in it; the important part lies in the fiction he was creating. Such a story implies both identifications with and alienations from the absent father, as well as the all-powerful mother and sister. More profoundly, it introduces the work of the imagination, breaking through familial blood-ties in order to disseminate affiliations beyond national boundaries.

The value of Poland is to serve as an agent of identity disruption. In a fragment written in 1822, Nietzsche insisted on the mixture of Polish and German blood in him. Nevertheless this fusion of bloodlines did not come about harmoniously: Each opposed the other, such that their host was divided, at least in two. According to Nietzsche's imagination, Polish blood is associated with rebellion: It favors individuality and genius, in opposition to the crowd and received opinion. Nietzsche's two Polish heroes were Copernicus and Chopin. The former had spent a good deal of time in Italy and came to contest the herd mentality by affirming that the earth orbited the sun. This astronomer is a prefiguration of Zarathustra, a freethinker who effects transmutations of knowledge. In addition to Copernicus's discovery of heliocentrism, Nietzsche remembered him for his ability to think against his own time and against his own self. But the Pole with whom he most identified remained Chopin, a fellow independent spirit who, Nietzsche held, liberated music from its German influences, especially Beethoven. The musical practice of Chopinian dissonance demonstrates the rebellion Nietzsche wished to glorify—a rebellion that also found political expression in this composer's patriotic revolt at the moment of the Warsaw Uprising of 1830. The Russian repression of the uprising made Chopin's exile definitive: He left Vienna for Paris and composed the Revolutionary Étude out of his spirit of resistance.

Nietzsche thus imagined himself as a brother to Chopin, and he sought confirmations in reality for this imagined relation. Didn't he have a Polish look about him, seen in both his character and his build? His friend Overbeck conceded this vanity, without truly believing it, considering such strange ancestry to be a mere game. But the degree of Nietzsche's conviction matters little: The point was to invent family resemblances through composition and through division. During his travels to Switzerland and Italy, Nietzsche took an adolescent pride at being mistaken for a Pole. And he considered these mistakes to be proofs of his imagined lineage, just like the summer at Marienbad or the winter at Sorrento, where people had even given him the nickname Il Polacco. His body thus betrayed his native lineage by exposing a second, deeper, and fundamentally foreign nature. Nietzsche had maintained this little family mythology for a long time, having played at it with his grandmother, who encouraged his fancy of being a Polish count. The collection of rumors, legends, anecdotes took shape in him to create a second nature that functioned as an antinature. Among his projective identifications, Italy limned an uprooted horizon, a choice of full sun with no shadow, whereas Poland reconstituted an origin, splitting that origin to better inscribe rebellion in his heart.

This recomposition of the self along nationalistic fantasies could have been limited to private phantasmagorias but became instead a creative force for Nietzsche. His reference to Chopin—which has been rather undervalued, indeed ignored by commentators—was not simply the object of a cultural identification on his part; it was also the very sound-matter that inspired him as a philosopher-musician. Nietzsche affirmed Chopin's absolute singularity, his inimitableness, in the history of music. Yet Nietzsche was himself attempting to create music following this "Polish" model. At eighteen, he composed a mazurka and a *csárdás*, which he offered to his sister Elisabeth "in memory of our Polish ancestors." Some twenty years later, he referred back to them again, remembering a dossier of mazurkas from his youth that he had written in memory of his ancestors. Upon close inspection, Nietzsche's mazurka is odd, set along a duple, not triple, meter. We might attribute this oddity to the apprentice-composer's youth. More interesting, however, is how this work almost plagiarizes its model, Chopin's Mazurka op. 7, no. 1. It takes its key, B flat, from its model, and despite the duple meter, the melody reproduces many of the original's developments almost exactly. Yet Nietzsche does not cite his source—as though he had been inspired by the same Polish vein that had inspired the original, as though he only needed access to the national folklore of that composition, but not the composition itself. Did he unconsciously copy Chopin? The question of whether Nietzsche plagiarized is not terribly pertinent; it fades away against the larger backdrop of his wider use of improvisation.

Nietzsche's piano playing mixed, in effect, performance, improvisation, and composition. He did not just play Chopin or Schumann: He played *with* them. Nietzsche was not content to sight-read a score, like a good amateur, nor did he aim for the art of some performative interpretation. Rather, he participated in the work and its world by re-creating it in his own manner. The young Friedrich immediately felt like a musician when, under the touch of his fingers, he discovered the composers he was studying. This proximity led him, without at all doubting the legitimacy of doing so, to improvise upon them, to give himself spontaneously over to invention, play, and composition. A multifaceted music lover, Nietzsche tested, recomposed, followed, and modified his sources. He allowed the world to enter through his ears, and, striking his diapason, determined what was good for his health, what would make him stronger. He likewise made use of this diapason on phi-losophers, reading and discussing Plato or Kant, wielding deri-sion and insult against them, but not without first having digested them, churning them about and regurgitating them. Nietzsche maintained a general dietetics applicable to food (he offered a good deal of alimentary advice: chocolate in the morning, no coffee; no alcohol; vegetables, but not too starchy; etc.) as well as to ideas and music. Eating, thinking, listening all required the same discrimina-tion in order to achieve good health. Learning music was a corpo-real experience through which he was nourished; it allowed him to develop and change. By playing certain composers, he caused the life forces within him to vibrate, leading him to be other than he had been taught to be. He even moved beyond these composers—no matter that he had not himself composed music at their level. He lived thanks to them and often against them, taking up that battle necessary to affirm one's own vitality.

As an improviser, Nietzsche was like a musical ogre who oozed back the harmonies he had devoured. At boarding school in Pforta, Nietzsche impressed his classmates by performing his pianistic in-spirations during storms. Among those classmates was Gersdorff, who remembered these evening improvisations in the music hall as imposing upon their listeners an entire private universe, a world of sounds and values, of images and feelings. The German language offers a word to describe such an atmosphere: *Stimmung*. It rings out, it resonates, it consonates, *es stimmt*, through the convocation and correspondence of multiple spiritual, sentimental, and sensual harmonies. Nietzsche's improvisation is tied to the creation of a *Stimmung*, either one in which the audience shares in the harmo-nies that move his tender soul or one that allows for his complete isolation as a musician withdrawn into his own lair of sound. It was thus during the scene, now famous, in which the young Nietzsche, finding himself in a Cologne brothel, headed straight to the salon's piano, improvised a piece, and then fled.

A great enthusiast for free improvisations, Nietzsche nevertheless wrote down many of his inspirations. The extent of the scores he left allows us to speak of him as a composer. He always had the ambition to become a renowned musician. But it would be a bit futile to analyze his musical production against the musical works of his time, for we would surely be limited to academic judgments about their shortcomings or mediocre plagiarisms. It would be more fruitful to look at them to see the different roles that music held in his life and his imagination. Among the some seventy compositions Nietzsche wrote, many remain incomplete. They reveal a range of projects, from instrumental music to vocal music, from symphonic pieces to choral works. Scarcely had he learned to play than the young Friedrich was already composing two sonatas for his mother. And then, upon refining his musical skill further, he composed a mass, a requiem, an oratorio, a miserere. A reader of Nietzsche's philosophy might be surprised to find so many musical works of religious inspiration. One hadn't imagined that the Antichrist composed masses! Nevertheless for Nietzsche, musical form exceeds all meaning, serving no particular message or spirituality. Instead, music contains worlds within it and thus engages existential values and life forces. Before making up his mind about music, Nietzsche first gleaned from the works of Mozart, Haydn, and Beethoven, producing a number of sketches in a rather anarchic and spontaneous manner. Nevertheless, his playing at the piano carried him clearly toward Romantic inspiration, which became the music he played with the greatest joy and which, in turn, became the music he most wanted to compose.

Before he began to systematically prefer Chopin over Schumann, relegating him to a folkloric Germanness, Nietzsche had insinuated himself into the latter composer's harmonies. The man he would later call the "mawkish Saxon" was one of the models for his early years, to the point that Nietzsche even placed flowers on Schumann's tomb upon arriving at Bonn to study philology. These were Nietzsche's Schumannian years, during which the piano accompanied his great moments of solitude. Schumann's music helped him pass the nights around the New Year's feast of St. Sylvester—those rendez-vous with time that Nietzsche always experienced as fateful. Eager to discover Schumann's works, Nietzsche read the scores for his orchestral pieces that had been reduced for the piano. He became particularly interested in *Manfred*, which his friend Gustav Krug had heartily recommended. This dramatic poem by Lord Byron, when linked to the piano, joined music to Romantic poetry and corresponded to the mood of Nietzsche the solitary student. It offered an expressive imagination into which he could project the states of his soul. The score for *Manfred* never left his music stand. It accompanied him during his moves—when he followed Ritschl, his tutor, to Leipzig, and then when he obtained a position at the University of Basel in 1869. The presence of this score in his life cannot be reduced to some anecdotal fetishism; rather, it constitutes the core of a complex affair in the musical life of Nietzsche as a composer. Playing *Manfred* at Bonn did not at all mean the same thing as playing it at Basel. In Switzerland, any association with Schumann underwent a contamination that was at once musical and emotional, a contamination that would feed the psychodrama of the relationship between Nietzsche and the Wagner couple. And the whole affair would play out around a score and a piano.

Ritschl had declared that he had never encountered such a genius as Nietzsche in his forty-year career. Now, as the new professor of classical philology at Basel, Herr Doktor Nietzsche could himself visit a genius, a composer whom he had discovered the year before: Richard Wagner. Wagner was living at Tribschen, on lake Lucerne, under the auspices of King Ludwig II of Bavaria; he gladly welcomed the rather young philosopher who might further advance his own stardom. He complimented Nietzsche's enthusiasm and made him believe that their friendship was exclusive. He encouraged Nietzsche to write *The Birth of Tragedy*, which would inscribe Wagner into the noble lineage of the Ancient Greeks. Nietzsche was swept away by Wagner's *Tristan*, as directed by Hans von Bülow, as well as by the overture of *Die Meistersinger*. And Nietzsche shared that same will to revolt incarnated by Wagner, which he felt could revolutionize not just music, but the very grammar of art. All of a sudden, his taste for Schumann became contested by his admiration for Wagner, who despised the patchwork of Romanticism and wanted to blow away all that preceded him. Nietzsche's musical playing and composing became the object of a knot tying together irreconcilables—a tension between private musical inspiration and his public and theoretical ambition. And the relationship between master and disciple became ever more complex as Wagner's wife also took it upon herself to rally this budding philosopher to their great cause by using her tried and true seductive powers.

This musical, philosophical, and sentimental intertwining found its ultimate expression in a musical composition for piano at which Nietzsche had been working during his years at Basel. This long work, titled *Manfred-Meditation*, clearly constitutes a reference to the Schumann work that he had played so often since his years at Bonn. But before Nietzsche's own work took its definitive form in 1872, its author had integrated, or ingested, lessons learned from Wagner, such that it would no longer be the fulfillment of a long association with the model of his youth, Schumann. In the meantime, Nietzsche had pledged himself to the Wagner couple and offered a small piano composition to Cosima for her birthday on the 25th of December 1871. Both the content and the circumstances around this gift are revelatory of the transformation Nietzsche had undergone; but they also reveal his illusions. He had in effect taken up a work composed eight years earlier, *Eine Sylvesternacht*, in order to make a new one titled *Nachklang einer Sylvesternacht*. The first version was written for violin and piano; the second, for piano four hands. Nietzsche was pleased and proud of the new work, which he played with his friend Overbeck before sending it to Cosima, anxious for her opinion.

One doesn't have to be a terribly sophisticated psychologist to understand that Nietzsche wanted to play the piano with Cosima sitting next to him and that he wished to enter into a certain harmony with her thanks to the score that he had composed for her. Twenty or so minutes together side by side one New Year's eve to usher in a new year and a new life. The work's new title is at once simple and enigmatic. *Echo of a New Year's Eve* clearly refers back to the original composition, *A New Year's Eve*, although Nietzsche doesn't indicate this, preferring the pretense of having composed a new work. Most of all, it is the word *echo* that remains ambiguous. It refers to a sound from the past, testifying to the persistence of melancholic feelings from his youth. Nietzsche entrusted this intimate bequest to Cosima: His moments of solitude and hope should resonate in the ears of his friend. On the other hand, an echo is also a sound that gets lost; we only hear its end, its extinction. This piece thus presents itself as the recognition of a before and an after: that which Nietzsche was, the son of Chopin and Schumann, and that which Nietzsche will be, the disciple of Wagner. The letters he wrote to his friends in which he spoke about this new work expose his contradictory feelings. In them, Nietzsche evoked a mixture of pain and triumph, of happiness and seriousness. And even though he had confessed to Krug that he had taken up a work from his youth, he insisted that its inspiration was radically new and a break from his early years. Of course Nietzsche expressed this tension in the philosophical terms that he was employing at the time: This musical event was a manifestation of the Dionysian, an upsetting of Apollonian restraint, along the lines of that influential binary at work in *The Birth of Tragedy*. Whatever the appropriate language needed to describe such a change might be, the recomposition of this piece reveals a problematic future for Nietzsche. He will search for himself and transform himself in a struggle with his contradictory points of reference, which will become echoes for him. And reality would indeed soon disillusion him of his stellar friendship with the genius and his wife: Cosima did not send back her opinion, but only a terse thank you with an allusion to the little bells used in this little piece of program music. Her letters to others reveal that she had had a good laugh with her husband, as well as her servant, over Nietzsche's musical pretenses.

Ambiguity and disappointment reached a new level with Nietzsche's *Manfred-Meditation*, finished in 1872; its vagueness was met with an official snub. Was it a Schumannian work? or a Wagnerian one? Specialists still debate the issue, with the likes of Florence Fabre privileging its Romantic allusion, and those like Éric Dufour revealing the motifs it took from Wagner's *Tristan*. In fact, this piece for piano four hands remains difficult to identify insofar as its endless chromaticisms do not allow a single form to be picked out. A certain pathos emerges from it, linking it to a few of the emotional atmospheres of some Schumannian works. But its destabilization of any tonal unity links it more readily to Wagner. Nietzsche seems to be in the throws of an internal conflict at the heart of his musical ambition—at once worked over by the Romantic vein in him and the expressive role reserved to music and, at the same time, attracted to a modern force of composition that freed itself from traditional harmonies and forms. Surely this indecision did not produce the work Nietzsche had hoped for. Instead it became subject to a judgment without appeal, which Nietzsche the apprentice-composer submitted himself to. He sent the score to Hans von Bülow, who was Cosima's former husband and, above all, the famous conductor of *Tristan* at Munich. Nietzsche accompanied the score with a long, obsequious letter in which he belittled his own musical talents. Such a tone might surprise a reader familiar with Nietzsche, who is used to more proud boastings. But at this moment, the future author of *Ecce Homo* was no more than a musician seeking recognition as a musician.

Misfortune must have guided Nietzsche's hand when he took up the very stick that would be used to beat him, for he got back far worse than would have been reasonable. Only a few days after the score was sent, Nietzsche received a scathing letter from von Bülow asking him if it had been a joke, so much had the parodic nature of the piece shocked his ears. If it was not a joke, he said that he was astonished that the most elementary rules of composition could be thus ignored. Von Bülow's nastiness went so far as to include an allusion to the Dionysian spirit that was so important to Nietzsche, observing that this work corresponded more to the day after a bacchanal: It was the result of a night of binging. The music was "detestable," a "rape," a "barbarous frenzy," a "crime against morality." The cruelest insult was surely against Nietzsche as a pianist, with von Bülow rejecting such "deplorable pianistic cramps." In short, return to your books and your philology, and end your interest in music! The *Manfred-Meditation*—the result of years of feelings, imaginings, and hopes—was thus reduced to a failed exercise. The wound Nietzsche received would never heal. Nevertheless the most interesting point here lies in the Wagnerian reference he slipped in between the lines. Von Bülow wondered whether his directing of *Tristan* had not made the young philosopher's head spin. And Nietzsche, rather than responding to the attack, apologized, expressed his mortification, renounced his youthful loves, blamed Romantic morbidity, and claimed that he would listen to *Tristan* for redemption. Later, however, he would transform this defeat through a process of psychological manipulation that took more care for his self-esteem: In *Ecce Homo*, he came back to von Bülow's harsh judgment, admitting that he had been brought up on Schumann's music. But he also declared that what he had composed was an "anti-Manfred," as though he had denounced such inspiration by pushing it to the extreme. His honor was thereby saved, and his reputation as a pianist and composer was thus not entirely compromised by the famous conductor's verdict. The Wagners had attempted to undo the blunder in order to return their potential disciple to their bosom. Cosima told him that he should have played the piece for them rather than sending it by mail. And Richard assured him, hypocritically, that Liszt had given his compositions a more favorable review.

Manfred's failure was at once both a poison and a revelation—although the truth for Nietzsche only revealed itself progressively and with the aid of several antidotes. We often reduce his conflict with Wagner to an affair of wounded pride. Instead, what was taking place was a violent moment of perceptiveness that permitted the philosopher-musician to find his own path. The deafening and venomous quarrel that led Nietzsche to denounce the composer he had so admired allowed him to come to understand which music suited him best and, more generally, which climate, which art, which culture fortified his being. The biographical grounds for this split are ultimately of little importance in comparison to the internal revolution that allowed him to understand that the Wagnerian influence was harmful to him. Wagner demanded the exclusiveness of his admirers. He could not tolerate that his would-be friend the philosopher had brought him the piano score to Brahms's *Triumphlied* when he himself had written a *Kaisermarsch*. This German genius in the making already had in mind the building of a theater worthy of his tetralogy, and his departure for Bayreuth and the triumphal success of the stagings of his *Ring* correspond inversely to Nietzsche's depression and exile to the Mediterranean. The philosopher had to hit bottom before finally being reborn: "To turn my back on Wagner was for me a fate; to like anything at all again after that, a triumph. Perhaps nobody was more dangerously attached to—grown together with—Wagnerizing; nobody tried harder to resist it; nobody was happier to be rid of it. A long story!—You want a word for it?—If I were a moralist, who knows what I might call it? Perhaps self-overcoming." Nietzsche's admission here merits greater attention. It cannot be reduced to a biographical confession: An entire politics of the body, and not just a personal disappointment, is at play in this adoption, and then rejection, of Wagner.

Against those commentators who tend to undervalue Nietzsche's polemical texts against Wagner, often reducing them to a personal settling of scores, I believe that they contain decisive stakes not just for music but also for defining a relationship to time through the playing of the piano. Throughout *Twilight of the Idols*, *The Case of Wagner*, and *Ecce Homo*, the attack against Wagner implies a critique on three levels: philosophical and historical; aesthetic and political; and psychological and physiological. The first stakes concern the age and the relationship between an individual and his times. From his own experience Nietzsche could ask: How can one have been Wagnerian and then later reject this inspiration? Precisely because, he explained, one had to be Wagnerian in order not to be so any longer, for Wagner was modernity itself. The "case" of Wagner thus goes beyond the composer and the musical tastes he inspired and encompasses the entire age. It was a break with tradition and a choice for the new. Nietzsche, who defined himself as the philosopher with a hammer, shared in the iconoclastic movement of modernity and in the will to be free. Nevertheless he warned of the danger that this emancipation might become the religion of the age, a discourse of progress that would corrupt the future with moral optimism. Nietzsche's care to discern the meaning behind profanation guided the whole of his analysis of Wagnerian modernity. Far from merely expressing a disappointed friendship, his texts demystify, through insults and humor, the seriousness that accompanied Wagner's modernist gestures. In his *Twilight of the Idols*, Nietzsche responded to Wagner's *Twilight of the Gods* by suggesting a decisive change: It is not sufficient to pull down ancient divinities; one must also attack the pedestals they stand on, the very grammar of thought that brings them forward. By lambasting Wagner in 1888, Nietzsche was aiming at both a new idol and a certain idea of modernity. He thereby set a joyful profanation against a serious revolution, an undisciplined modernity against a redemptive newness. In his own manner, Nietzsche was asking the question, "What does it mean to be modern?" His response entailed a way of relating to time: We have to accept our times but also fight against that which makes us products of our times. "Through Wagner modernity speaks most intimately, concealing neither its good nor its evil—having forgotten all sense of shame. And conversely: One has almost completed an account of the value of what is modern once one has gained clarity about what is good and evil in Wagner. I understand perfectly when a musician says today: 'I hate Wagner, but I can no longer endure any other music.' But I'd also understand a philosopher who would declare: 'Wagner sums up modernity. There is no way out, one must first become a Wagnerian.'" The break was thus complete, and it had to be accepted because modernity corresponded to the future. But Nietzsche, unlike Hegel, did not see this as the fulfillment of an objective and necessary Spirit. Instead he stood in a posture of defiance against his own times. To be of one's times did not mean being in accord with the moment. Wagner was the modern-as-contemporary. According to Nietzsche, what mattered was thus to begin by being Wagnerian in order to then sacrifice the idol that the times had erected and that was subjugating the future to Progress. In a way, he invites us to profane the profaners once they have become in turn symbols of their own times. And the instrument to achieve this necessary iconoclasm would be, for Nietzsche, the diapason hammer, with the piano as a scale for evaluation.

Thinking is an affair of the ear. So what can we hear about time when listening to Wagner's tetralogy? Any critique here becomes aesthetic and political. Nietzsche had the extreme prescience to understand—before Adorno, Benjamin, or Arendt—that totalitarianism manifests itself in systems of language and forms of art. Musical aesthetics involves different levels of listening, systems, and feelings that engage a particular understanding of the individual and of society. In Wagner's music, Nietzsche perceived a communal belief, or even faith: Siegfried became a revolutionary figure, in the spirit of the harbingers of 1789. The modernist break with its old gods had lost its creative value and dissolved into the hope of a "redemption" for both man and art.

Through Wagnerian music, Nietzsche attacked the very grammar of the sacred. He thereby carried out a project of sap digging, throwing doubt onto the images and rhythms of modernity, without, for all that, himself becoming conservative. His tactical profanations, organized around the case of Wagner, offered a merciless lucidity that would detect any resurgence of the sacred—and its metaphysics—at work in the key discourses of modernity, no matter how sacrilegious such discourses seemed. The principal traits of this grammar of the sacred include symbolic infusion, overdramatization, and ostentation. Nietzsche denounced the will toward loftiness, which was so typical of Wagnerian idealism, along with its corollaries: a taste for the infinite, a search for purity, the illusion of "after-worlds." Against any semiotics of sound in the service of transcendence, summed up by "boom-boom symbolism," Nietzsche worked a devastating rapprochement: Wagner is the Victor Hugo of music for having transformed it into language. The symbolization of music requisitions every sound in order to make signs out of those sounds and then to overinvest them with allegorical meaning. The grammar of the sacred is thereby entirely directed toward its audience. Idealism itself is a spectacle that works on feelings (of immensity, of profundity, of the infinite) in order to promote the great imposture of a beyond. Wagnerian music is overdramatized; "Teutonic schlock" prevails over the music. ("Wagner is an actor who neither composes nor thinks as a musician.") Nietzsche intuited the appropriation of this music into a politics of the sacred, which would erect a State, an Idea, or some other idol. At the time he was writing, Nietzsche could only draw comparisons to Hegel, but he knew how to detect the kinship between this grammar of the sacred and the construction of the Reich. Under this same spirit of obedience, the statesman becomes the orchestral conductor of the weak: "Wagner's stage requires one thing only—*Teutons!*—Definition of the Teuton: obedience and long legs.—It is full of profound significance that the arrival of Wagner coincides in time with the arrival of the '*Reich*.'"

To his philosophical and historical critique, and aesthetic and political critique, Nietzsche added another that blended psychology and physiology. This third critique allowed him to understand Wagner's success. And it was from Nietzsche's own history of sickness and recovery that he, the philosopher with a piano-diapason, would make Wagner into a medical case study. Nietzsche went back to an analysis he had developed at length about metaphysicians and priests, about Socratic philosophy and Judeo-Christian religion. He showed how these would-be healers were in fact those who infected others with disease. They claim, as Socrates had, to deliver humanity from its earthly misery by leading them to an ideal and illusory sacredness. Weak and incapable of enjoying life themselves, they seek to convince others to love weakness by holding out for them empty spiritual compensations. Wagner followed in this metaphysical tradition, and through his sonorous heights, he set traps for philosophers who are all too ready to prefer the sublime over beauty. The sacred had, in effect, taken refuge in the sublime; Kant had described its supernatural motifs in the contemplation of storms on mountain tops. In the sublime, Nietzsche noted, philosophers could find a substitute for the decline of divine transcendence, and the masses could give themselves over to the colossal exaltation of popular art. More generally, this psychological critique attacks false profundities—whether musical or conceptual—which are founded on the sacralization of the ineffable. (These false depths would later be denounced by Freud and Wittgenstein.) In the Wagnerian sublime, one no longer dances, but soars. Nietzsche attacked the new dogmas of Wagnerian music, criticizing *Parsifal* for promoting a spirit of sacralization that covered over the melody in favor of orchestral harmony alone. Nietzsche the psychologist offered his diagnosis as an opposition to this music: "Wagner's art is sick. The problems he presents on the stage—all of them problems of hysterics—the convulsive nature of his affects, his overexcited sensibility, his taste that required even stronger spices, his instability that he dressed up as principles, not least of all the choices of his heroes and heroines—consider them as psychological types (a pathological gallery)!—all of this taken together represents a profile of sickness that permits no further doubt. *Wagner est une névrose*—'Wagner is a neurosis.'"

Nietzsche's critique of Wagner took place during years of productivity and was motivated by a reclaiming of his self and an affirmation of vital joy. His conception of music changed radically, becoming far removed from his first considerations in *The Birth of Tragedy* and the artistic metaphysics it still contained. Starting from an ever more physical musical playing, Nietzsche modified his relation to musical ecstasy. From then on, his critique developed along physiological grounds, evaluating music according to its benefits for the body, understood as a life force. Wagner's oeuvre, with its tonal indeterminacies and continuous melody, stimulates the nerves; it is at once intoxicating and befuddling. "He's a nervous breakdown who targets other sick people to make them even sicker." Continuing his dietary considerations, Nietzsche likens the effects of this music to alcoholic beverages, which cause a degeneration of one's sense of rhythm. Indeed, Wagner sought these very effects and worked to wear down any resistance to them in order to plunge his listeners into an "oceanic feeling." Emblematic of a sick age, Wagner was a healer who further sickened already exhausted bodies. Nietzsche's denunciation of the weak does not hide the fact that he too was one of the admirers who had succumbed to this composer's charm. In *Ecce Homo*, the metaphor adequate to describe the Wagnerian aroma becomes hashish: "I could not have endured my youth without Wagner's music. For I was condemned to Germans. If one wants to rid oneself of unbearable pressure, one needs hashish. Well then, I needed Wagner." For so impassioned a young man as Nietzsche, who wanted to distance himself from his German roots and who was thus open to new sensations, Wagner's music was a therapeutic substance. But again, the remedy itself becomes a poison if, rather than healing, it only gets a person used to the disease. Little by little, Nietzsche came to realize just how much this euphoria had become the national opium he wanted to flee. The references to Germanic myths in Wagner's music horrified him: The climate of dark, damp forests was, after all, harmful to his physical and mental constitution. Such music oozed the collective feeling of the *Heimat*, of belonging to ancestral roots. It could not suit Nietzsche.

The Wagnerians never gave any credit to these Nietzschean diagnoses. If and when they read his works, they saw in them only superfluous rhetoric and bad faith. Nevertheless Nietzsche's considerations are not without value even for today's reader. By doing philosophy with his ears and by adopting the piano-diapason as his touchstone for political and aesthetic systems, Nietzsche learned how to distinguish, starting with Wagner, the values and qualities of modernity. But it is one thing to undertake the necessary act of delivering oneself from the power of idols and another to believe oneself capable of curing the masses. By insulting Wagner, Nietzsche had begun a genealogical critique that allowed him to identify the metaphysical grammar of a salvific modernity. Its lexicon, its syntax, and its figures all implicitly promote a separation between: the here and the beyond; the ear and the word; and the body and the soul. Today such a critique remains of great value because it exhausts the deadlocked, obsessional oppositions between conservatism and modernity. It dismisses both the illusions of the sacred (its false depths; the intoxication of the sublime) and the clear conscience of the profane (positivism; self-satisfied hedonism). It renders obsolete both traditionalism (reverence for the ancients; deference to past authority) and presentism (naive devotion to the new; the transgressive gestures of the avant-gardists, formerly futurists, which have since become merely a sales pitch for the continued replacement of consumer goods). Above all, the striking of this diapason sketches out a different modernity: a joyful, circumstantial, and anticonformist modernity—one that is not an act of purification but a scratching off, a defiance that refuses to be taken in. Treating Wagner as a "case study" is thus to perform a reevaluation of culture and to undertake a fierce, mean profanation against any possible resurgence of seriousness.

From this life-saving act of sobering up, Nietzsche discovered three antidotes during the years 1881, 1882, and 1883. Their names were Carmen, Salomé, and Zarathustra. Each allowed him to find the languages and forms appropriate to his musical, as well as philosophical, needs. His own piano compositions could not synthesize Romantic melody and Wagnerian orchestration. Nietzsche did much better in the pieces where voice, accompaniment, rhythm, and tonality were clearly distinguished. His departure for the Mediterranean and his stays in Genoa, Rome, Venice, and Nice afforded him the opportunity to hear the music of different composers, like Rossini or Bellini. It was love at first sight when Nietzsche attended an 1881 production of *Carmen* in Genoa (and in Italian), which brought together for him France, Spain, and Italy. The passion he felt for Bizet's opera corresponded perfectly to his personal metamorphosis and the therapy he so vitally needed. Some commentators believe that Nietzsche was exaggerating here, but it is beyond doubt that he loved this work: he listened to it compulsively and on every possible stage. At the opera in Nice he went to see it several times in a row. He procured the score so he could try it out on every piano available to him. Nietzsche thereby administered to himself the medicine he needed. His score of *Carmen* is covered with annotations, testifying to his intense appropriation of the opera to the piano.

The piano remained his diapason and laboratory table. He would transcribe what he heard and what he liked. And for Nietzsche the musician, transcription means transvaluation. Playing *Carmen* allowed him to purge himself, to nourish himself anew, to transform himself. Musicologists, of course, will smile at such a grotesque choice: One would have to be crazy to prefer Bizet to Wagner! But Nietzsche's musical passion constituted both a subjective medication and a tactic of war. He was not launching a new *Querelle des Bouffons* (the eighteenth-century *Quarrel of the Comic Actors*); he wasn't replacing Wagner with Bizet. Had he wanted to have the debate solely on aesthetic grounds, he would have chosen Rossini. And deep down inside him, the combat pitted Wagner against Schumann. Moreover, if he had to describe his ideal composer, one who would remain unchallenged throughout his life, it would have been Chopin. With Bizet, Nietzsche defended the inspiration shared by the "Polish" composer for the bel canto— song for song's sake, song that was polished and relieved of the burden of meaning. *Carmen*'s creator allowed him to unite Italy, France, and Poland—all of which were alternatives to Germany.

Above all, *Carmen* offered Nietzsche a musical antidote. Beneficial to his health, its music had a healing power by manifesting a different orientation and a different space in which life and thought could be united: "Yesterday I heard—would you believe it?—Bizet's masterpiece, for the twentieth time. Again I stayed there with tender devotion; again I did not run away. This triumph over my impatience surprises me. How such a work makes one perfect! One becomes a 'masterpiece' oneself. Really, every time I heard *Carmen*

I seemed to myself more of a philosopher, a better philosopher, than I generally consider myself: So patient do I become, so happy, so Indian, so settled." Music is appreciated from a physiological and therapeutic point of view. It speaks to both body and soul, which Nietzsche does not distinguish. He maintains that the world enters through our ears and that our understanding requires a unique act of listening. Temperament, moods, ideas, passions— all are mobilized by music. And Bizet's music, simplistic though it appears to learned music lovers, produces as many feelings as it does thoughts. Indeed, its virtue lies in not proclaiming its own intelligibility, in not demanding any commentary or theory. "And, oddly, deep down I don't think of it, or don't know how much I think about it."

To think is to hear, and music teaches the philosopher to become a better "listener." In a nonreflexive way, music contains the sensible world. It lives through the ears that absorb it, and our ears are thus able to make the whole presence of this life of becoming resonate. Far from any "lies of grand style" or learned discourses, music listened to under Mediterranean light fosters a different kind of relation to the earth: pleasure; frivolity; *limpidezza*; a dry climate. Having broken with all that Germany exuded, Nietzsche exalted the "tanned and scorched sensibility" of France, Italy, and Spain—even the joyfulness of North Africa (remarks later repressed by his Nazi inheritors). In *The Case of Wagner*, Nietzsche shattered not only the idol Wagner but also his Germanic pedestal by declaring—in French: "*Il faut méditerraniser la musique.*" ["Music must be Mediterranianized."] This exhortation goes beyond any opposition between *Carmen* and *Parsifal*, or even beyond any strictly musicological debate. Is there indeed even any sense in accusing Nietzsche of bad taste, of bias, or of some thirst for revenge? One should have the conviction of one's tastes, and, even more so, of one's bad tastes. For Nietzsche, the physiological stakes of music outweigh any strictly aesthetic consideration. Or rather, the aesthetics engaged by the body, which listens and thinks at the same time, transcends all form.

The Salomé antidote belongs above all to a sentimental register. Nietzsche's disappointed love for Lou Salomé has given rise to many more or less romanticized tales. Nevertheless this relationship had an equally important effect on Nietzsche's piano playing and composition. With *Carmen* the point was to play Bizet's work at the piano in order to become filled by it. With Lou, Nietzsche composed music in order to accompany the words of his loved one. He took up the *lied* again, a form he had experimented with in the style of Schubert, following a genre much prized in Germany. From the age of seventeen, Nietzsche had attempted to combine poetic lyrics with piano music, composing over a dozen *lieder*. One poem given to him by Lou provided the opportunity to go back to this musical vein. This time he would no longer be attempting to inscribe it into a tradition of vocal music; instead, he would compose a personal and confessional work. Once again Nietzsche took up an old composition and reworked it with a new addressee in mind. In 1874, he had written a piece for piano four hands, titled *Hymn to Friendship*. It had been intended for use in an orchestral version developed from texts his friends were supposed to produce. The title itself displayed a creative euphoria: Nietzsche had taken his inspiration from Greek songs, hymns, and dithyrambs—showing an enthusiasm for divine figures. Seeking to vanquish his Wagnerian disillusionments and the failure of *Manfred*, he had felt the need to re-create a community of friends to whom he could dedicate a song. Gersdorff and Rohde were the recipients of this new impulse, which signaled Nietzsche's recovery of a joy for life. Beethoven's *Ode to Joy*, with due allowances, underlies his declaration that this composition would finally be free of regretful meanderings. The piece, however, would forever remain in its pianistic form.

Lou's poem "Prayer to Life" stirred in Nietzsche a desire to compose once again and to link their two names in a single work. This work would synthesize music and poetry, mapping out the stellar uniting of Lou and Friedrich. The substance of the poem is this: One should love life for both the happiness and misery it produces. As such, Nietzsche's love was required to elevate it to the level of a great tragic poem. But the poetic quality of the text matters little: Its *amor fati* and its *yes* to life were declared openly and thus could resonate with the harmonies composed by the philosopher. He adapted the poem to the meter of the *Hymn to Friendship*, composing, in 1882, the *lied* titled *Prayer to Life*. The work could have remained there, as the work of two people, as the love affaire of Lou and Friedrich, who could sit apart from Paul Rée while playing their piece together: a duo to break the trinity that had caused Nietzsche to suffer so. But his ambition carried him away from the intimate sharing of a collaborative work. Perhaps it was the thirst for revenge against Wagner that drove him to enlarge the piece. Nietzsche wanted to transform it into a choral work to be played in public. His friend Köselitz, aka Peter Gast, wrote an orchestration, since Nietzsche himself remained a pianist and had not mastered the techniques for such a composition. He even hoped to have it performed by the chorus directed by Professor Riedel, whom he had known at Leipzig. But the project would never come to be. Still, despite his break with Lou, Nietzsche would later publish the score at his own expense. He even referred to it regularly in his correspondence, declaring that it replaced all of his prior compositions and that it was in fact his last will and testament to be played upon his death.

The third antidote did not, properly speaking, produce a musical work, but was inspired through and through by listening to and playing music. The project of writing *Thus Spoke Zarathustra* had already been present in the other two antidotes, *Carmen* and Salomé. In fact, the three remedies or antidotes were mixed together into a complex concoction. Listening to *Carmen*, meeting Lou Salomé, and conceiving *Zarathustra* all nourished Nietzsche's body and mind from 1881 on. They follow along with his Mediterranean peregrinations, alternating between love at first sight and disappointment, at times merging love, writing, and opera. Without doubt it was music that governed the flow of these metamorphoses. Nietzsche walked, composed, desired, became excited, and wrote from a musical vein for which the foundation would remain the piano—the instrument that he would never abandon even when he had ceased all other activities. And it was thus with *Zarathustra*: The celebrated vision of Surlei, which was the origin of this work, cannot be reduced to the revelation of an intelligible truth. Rather, it overwhelmed Nietzsche in a flash of music and it gave the philosophical poem-to-be an essentially musical dimension, understood as a song that exceeds verbal meaning. The philosopher himself suggested as much in *Ecce Homo*:

> Perhaps the whole of *Zarathustra* may be reckoned as music; certainly a rebirth of the art of *hearing* was among its preconditions. In a small mountain spa not far from Vicenza, Recoaro, where I spent the spring of 1881, I discovered together with my maestro and friend, Peter Gast, who was also "reborn," that the phoenix of music flew past us with lighter and more brilliant feathers than it had ever displayed before. But if I reckon forward from that day to the sudden birth that occurred in

February 1883 under the most improbable circumstances—the *finale* from which I have quoted a few sentences in the Preface was finished exactly in that sacred hour in which Richard Wagner died in Venice—we get eighteen months for the pregnancy. This figure of precisely eighteen months might suggest, at least to Buddhists, that I am really a female elephant.

For Nietzsche, metaphors have a decisive importance. They prevail over the very concepts for which they establish meaning. In this story of giving birth, the phoenix indicates a rebirth of the philosopher-musician. The story caused an *élan vital* to resurface within him and provided him a symbolic value upon the death of Wagner in Italy. The composer from Bayreuth had also died in him—in his new, Mediterranean body. And the actual date of Wagner's death sealed this transformation that had begun with Nietzsche's departure from Germany. The comparison of *Thus Spoke Zarathustra* to a symphonic poem cannot be reduced to an analogy between philosophical poetry and music. Instead, it describes the metamorphosis of a philosopher-artist in physiological terms. Nietzsche had held that Bizet's *Carmen* made him a better philosopher because it made him a better listener. *Zarathustra* established a new way of listening that afforded a better way to hear the language of the world. To the decadence of Wagnerian modernity, Nietzsche now opposed an auditory regeneration. Through this personal mythology, he described an internal disturbance that would bring about a palingenesis. Rather than any divine inspiration by which Romantics or metaphysicians account for the "birth" of a work *ex nihilo*, the philosopher-artist asserts that we create from a corporeal alchemy that transforms lead into gold. The philosopher-artist transforms into a matrix, a womb ready to give birth, combining male and female to deliver that which would deliver him. The phoenix is the ethereal and luminous sign that presides over the transmutation at once engendered and received by the creator, who becomes at once the subject and object of such an event. While *Zarathustra* presents three metamorphoses (the camel, the lion, and the child), Nietzsche here proposes a fourth, the elephant cow, which comes to represent the salvific remedy that he pursued at the risk of physical and mental chaos.

The story of this gestation confirms the physiological musicality of Nietzsche's *Zarathustra*. It unfolds over three moments and three Mediterranean locations. A winter in the bay of Rapallo presided over the first songs. In Rome, the second location, Nietzsche heard a tune that would haunt him and remain with his work. Oddly, he never sought to transcribe this melancholic song, referring to it as the *Nachtlied*. The few words that constitute its refrain were given as the "death of immortality." To be sure, the composition of *Zarathustra* was a struggle, a constant effort at "good health" against the resurgence of Nietzsche's morbid tendencies. Whatever the case may be, this interior song came to be expressed in the words of a philosophical poem, and not as a piano piece or proper *lied*. As an antidote, *Zarathustra* offers a third kind of Nietzschean musical practice when compared to his lyrical listening of *Carmen* or to his collaborative composition with Lou Salomé. Without doubt *Zarathustra* corresponds better to the philosopher's victory over his past defeats, and its subsequent history has borne this out. *Thus Spoke Zarathustra* is a song of praise, a successful climb, a summit reached after so many uncertain ascents. The third and final part of his writing Nietzsche associated with the walks he took near Nice on a path that led him from the train station at Èze to the fortified town above, which overhangs the Mediterranean. Many philosophers have since taken this same steep path, which now carries the name of its famous trailblazer; at least one has even lost his life doing so. The climb affords luminous views through the rocks, which join to form a V. Nietzsche was clearly associating his own muscular strength and joyful enthusiasm with the new possibilities he was setting out for the Superman: "Often one could have seen me dance; in those days I could walk in the mountains for seven or eight hours without a trace of weariness. I slept well, I laughed much—my vigor and patience were perfect." Once at the top of the path, he would gaze at the midday sky with its unrivaled light, as though it offered a Mediterranean response to the paintings by Caspar Friedrich. The misty heights of the German Romantics were transformed by this wandering exile into luminous rock. He was at last joyful among the cypresses and cistuses.

That Nietzsche's regeneration was owed to his *Zarathustra* might lead one to think that poetic writing gave him the best antidote to resolve his musical themes and hopes. Nevertheless, we cannot forget that Nietzsche, despite his disappointment as a composer, continued to think of himself—and to dream of himself—as a musician more than as a philosopher or poet. The piano constituted a focal point from which all of his ambitions shone forth. At the piano, he entered into a dialogue with his favorite musicians, from Bach to Bizet. It was there that he improvised and composed at the whim of his infatuations, from Schumann and Chopin to Wagner. And it was there that he dreamed up the tunes to accompany cherished lyrics. He always found himself at the piano in moments of great solitude, including after his definitive break from all human contact. And even his years of intense philosophical writing never eclipsed his desire to be a musician—the very desire that had been forged in his youth, when he was torn between theology and music. After having written his *Zarathustra*, and indeed after having written his major works, he regularly confided to his friend Peter Gast that he would above all liked to have been a musician.

And the older he got, the more he expressed his regret at this failure, finding consolation only in playing the piano and belittling his own intellectual production. Since only his *Hymn to Life* had been published, Nietzsche remained the only performer of his own works. The friends to whom he dedicated his scores hardly ever followed his example. It would be too easy to consider his philosophical writing as compensation for his musical projects, or to describe it by analogy as "thoughtful music," even if he sometimes referred to his books in terms of a musical score. Nietzsche did at times entertain abandoning the piano and renouncing music for the sake of his philosophy. Intrigued by the invention of the typewriter, there was a time when he employed his fingers exclusively on that keyboard of letters. Nevertheless music was not a hobby that he could abandon without consequence. Like his walks and midday contemplations, music was a vital activity for—and even indispensable to—his good health.

Music is more than a mere comparison or model; it offers a time and a scale for evaluation. It provides a list of rules and a sounding board with which Nietzsche was able to think auditorily about the world. Moving philosophy beyond the privileging of the eye, just as so many twentieth-century philosophers would do, Nietzsche used his unique diapason to hear systems of thought, authors, and cultures and to evaluate them against his own piano playing, harmonies, and songs. Was not the hammer he brandished against idols at first the hammer that struck the strings of this familiar instrument? The question of coherence between Nietzsche the philosopher and Nietzsche the musician has been the object of much writing because his musical conceptions varied, depending on whether he was emphasizing creation, reception, or music itself—sometimes he was a Romantic, sometimes a physiologist, and sometimes a formalist. Nevertheless, his writings on music and his musical compositions do not always hold together, since they were affected by circumstantial influences or climates. Writing about music, playing music, and composing music do not obey the same rhythms or feelings. Any attempt at an *a posteriori* synthesis would cover over their unique qualities. More than a philosopher of music, Nietzsche was a philosopher-musician, and in particular a philosopher-pianist. The choice of this instrument was important not only to his playing of music but also to his thinking about music, especially for one who wished to recall the corporeal foundation of all creation.

It was at the piano that Nietzsche experienced, tested, and developed the vibrations that threw his character and his thoughts into such upheaval. He often remarked that he had been swept away by this piece of music or by that improvisation. In alternation, he found at the piano pain and joy, moderation and excess, nuance and force. As an interpreter of ancient Greece, he articulated these tensions as the opposition between Apollo and Dionysus. And while we remember that he denounced the suffocation of the Dionysian by reason, wisdom, Socratic or Christian morality, etc., these two principles found a balance in the best of creations, whether in tragedy, opera, or philosophy. And piano playing is precisely an activity that requires conjoining the uniqueness of the performer with a respect for the score. The exceedingly few observations that Nietzsche made about piano playing, which can be found in his *Fragments*, call for a nonimpulsive fingering and recommend regular practice—the only means to control the desire to express oneself. Even when he improvised, allowing himself to follow his fits of creativity, Nietzsche respected the meter and brought his inspiration into a regulating tempo. From time to time, he would catch himself going beyond the prescribed order and be surprised by the unexpected result. For he had not simply slipped in between the notes composed by Schumann or Chopin; instead such excess was a sign of his emancipation from older forms. He took delight in this excess, just as he would congratulate himself for going beyond established moral values. Excess was not, however, an uncontrolled fit that leads to a false note or that calls for a scream in the middle of the melody. All art consists in transforming impulses and excessive impetus, with the help of a rhythm or harmony that conserves the tension between force and balance. It is striking to observe how Nietzsche articulated these opposing poles just as much in his piano playing as in his life and philosophy. He employed the same terms for them all, as in *Ecce Homo*, where he describes philosophical inspiration: "One is altogether beside oneself, with the distinct consciousness of subtle shudders and of one's skin creeping down to one's toes; [. . .] an instinct for rhythmic relationships that arches over wide spaces of forms—length, the need for a rhythm with wide arches, is almost the measure of the force of inspiration, a kind of compensation for its pressure and tension." Thanks to rhythm, the tears that rattled the thinker and musician are converted into joy, and the body, laid low by so much emotion, can dance again on light feet.

The piano was thus more than an "instrument" for Nietzsche because it could not be reduced to a mere means of expression. It became a place for sound in which the philosopher-musician could find his values, scales, and intensities. A vector for the feelings that went through his body and mind, it fixed an equilibrium point and a line of continuity when great intellectual and sentimental fractures shattered his plans for the future. Through the piano, the philosopher concocted dialogues with his preferred interlocutors—those musicians whose sonorous thought inspired him more than the thought of the metaphysicians. Through it he dreamed of glory, wanting to make his mark on history as a composer. The piano was at once a center and a space. It played a central role as a forge for evaluation and organization by taking the vibrations of his thoughts, dreams, and desires into its sound box. It selected those sounds that were most promising for the unfolding of rhythms and for the emergence of a "style" that would be incommensurable to any style, relying heavily on variations and tensions. It offered Nietzsche a unique time and singular activity, even if everything passed through it. It presented him with an activity somewhere between listening and writing. When he went to hear an opera or symphonic concert, he gave himself over to a total digestive experience, as though he were imbibing a sonorous substance capable of transforming him. His compulsive listening to *Carmen*, or his being reduced to tears after concerts testify to this experience. On the other hand, his philosophical writing was governed by a will to assert his singularity, to overtake the herd. Nietzsche presented himself in these writings as the pitiless critic or solitary prophet, marking a rupture in the history of Western thought with his different patronymics. Between these two attitudes of ingestion and exclamation, piano playing was a middle ground or intersection. Whether as an interpreter, improviser, or composer, Nietzsche played over and over the music he appropriated. More than a mere performer, but less than an inventor, he constantly reworked what was pleasing to his ears. A keen transcriber of music, he rediscovered the works he had heard in concert on his own keys, thereby re-appropriating for himself the music that had delighted him to the point of paroxysm. By playing these pieces again, he became his own conductor in his own rhythm. He could follow, correct, or move this or that motif. An improviser and composer to varying degrees, he participated in the harmony of reception and recomposition. Through the piano, Nietzsche used music the way Montaigne, one of his favorite thinkers, had taken up ancient authors: Once digested by our bodies, their ideas belong to us. Nietzsche let the world in through his ears to the point of indigestion, and when language could no longer tie him to reality, the piano remained his enduring diapason.

Èze, Summer 2007

Four

THE PIANO TOUCHES ME

The word *amateur* in French has an ambivalent set of meanings. It can refer equally well to the discriminating connoisseur or to the approximating amateur. An *amateur de piano* is a connoisseur of pianos, one who knows how to pick out a worthy instrument in terms of both its sound and its mechanics. Such an *amateur* is able to evaluate the hammers, the soundboard, and so on. She can distinguish among brands and even identify the materials and place of origin of a piano's construction. An *amateur au piano*, on the other hand, is defined by his shortcomings. This type of *amateur* only plays from time to time, without fully mastering piano technique. Content with browsing through musical scores and bringing a tune to life, he never gets around to polishing the pieces he plays. Dilettantism is the more elevated version of this casual approach. Its ease derives from the whim and peregrinating pleasure of the occasional player: Why not have a bit of piano this evening? Why not put my maladroit fingers to a few melodies? The lower version of such a casual approach is amateurism: the pretension of wanting to touch the keys without having the means to do so. Through poor fingering and a lack of rhythm, this half-hearted player is condemned to playing at home—he wouldn't be able to play anywhere else, unless some immodesty leads him to believe in his own untapped talent. He would nevertheless remain an "amateur." The pejorative connotations of amateurism rest on the simple distinction between the professional, who lives through his playing, and the amateur, who only plays for his pleasure. But this opposition becomes a little more complicated when we attempt to understand abilities and practices that are less clear-cut. Was Nietzsche an amateur? We would hesitate to define him as such: His remarkable playing made him much more than a week-end pianist. He seems worthy of the professional level. Still, if our only criterion is mastery of the musical instrument, it remains difficult to fix the level at which a pianist leaves amateurism behind. Conservatory examinations or competitions provide only relative scales. We should, no doubt, approach amateurism through a means of evaluation other than technique. Then we can observe amateurism's unique relation to a particular kind of music and a particular kind of instrument.

Roland Barthes played the piano daily; he was also a "connoisseur," an expert of musicology. But he wished to maintain a clear distinction between his writing and his playing. These two activities could, of course, be linked—even desirably so, since understanding a performance by playing the piece ourselves brings an internal knowledge to our musical analysis. Musicologists "read" scores in light of their own experience. Those few philosophers who have dared to speak about music without such a personal understanding of it are condemned to proffering mere generalities. Rousseau, Nietzsche, Wittgenstein, Adorno, Sartre, Jankélévitch were not of this type; they all knew how to read, play, and analyze a musical score. Yet the relations between their musical playing and their musicological writing did not follow the same paths, especially when their private tastes differed strongly from their aesthetic speculations. A large gap between playing and writing is not necessarily evidence of an internal contradiction or secret. Rather, it underlines a dissociation among registers. Nietzsche discussed Wagner but played Chopin; Sartre too loved Chopin, although he would more readily offer his opinions on Schoenberg. The playing of music and the writing of musicology are at once separate yet linked. One can write about one composer but play another; one can also play the music one writes about, as was the case with Adorno or Jankélévitch; or indeed one can write about the music one plays. Barthes chose this third path, albeit in an amusingly paradoxical way: He affirmed the radical difference between playing and discussing music yet wrote about his own piano playing. Indeed, his writings initiate a shift in musicology toward an analysis of practice—a shift that is even more marked because he considered amateur practices. In his texts, the amateur's playing implements feelings and temporalities that elude the pejorative, or perhaps merely underestimating, definition of amateurism. The amateur is not a lesser pianist, but a pianist who plays differently!

When Roland Barthes spoke about his own musical playing, to a certain extent he evoked the musical playing of any and everyone. His comments speak to the experience of the anonymous pianist who indulges in his instrument without worrying about the result. Such an amateur brings to his playing a variety of different relationships—sonorous, corporeal, affective, spiritual, and so on. But how can we take all these private and personal behaviors into account? There are such a variety of amateurs that it seems impossible to derive any synthesis from among the choices each makes: whether to use a musical score; whether to improvise; whether to play an hour every day, or to really get down to it only when inspiration strikes; whether to play alone or with the family; whether to add electronics; whether to be accompanied by other instruments; and so on. Better, no doubt, to begin by analyzing oneself and one's own musical playing and then to try to find those truths felt by others as well. This attempt to found a science of the individual had been Barthes's impossible ambition when writing about photography. Yet the piano engages its player far more than images engage their viewer. The piano accompanies its player throughout his entire life, with regularity, from learning to play as a child to the point where playing becomes an activity that is both reflected and commented upon. The piano is at once a rhythm and a duration. To speak of oneself at the piano implies going through one's entire existence, like a biography sketched out across a musical spectrum. Barthes himself was known for being reticent about giving his life story. He preferred to diffract *biographemes*—those quanta of a life story—in order to spin out the flow of personal time. On his inner piano there lay a score in pieces, like random fragments of music that can be played differently, depending on their sequence. Feelings and ideas become inscribed on that inner score as marks or traces, either to be struck or erased—without any way for us to fit them into some linear measure.

The writings of Barthes on playing music as an amateur are not, at first sight, coherent. Rather, they seem to extend the experience of music into more speculative discourse. Based on the idea of a shifting subjectivity, Barthes's theoretical intention comes close to being impossible. But he was careful not to construct a full philosophical aesthetics—even if he did develop a little philosophy of amateurism, for one has to be a bit of a philosopher in order to explain what is at play in the relationships between the body and time, touch, and sound. Barthes's reflections are not contained in some grand treatise on the subject. Instead, they are developed here and there, as light touches through which he conveys his pleasure of playing. He follows this pleasure into writing and analyzes it in the manner of both a phenomenologist and a psychologist. Barthes's movement toward theoretical generality develops through the personal description of his tastes, his sensitivity, indeed his sexuality, all of which are linked to the piano. Besides listening to and reading music, there is also the inner playing of music, which carries with it a sensual understanding of the music. The piano player's ears and eyes cannot overshadow his hands or fingers; through them his body expresses and constructs the music. This mixture of registers—learned and personal, systematic and sentimental—has given rise to some confusion among those who expected Barthes to provide a discourse more clearly identifiable by its discipline—perhaps musicology, semiology, or sociology. Barthes is still accused today of intellectual impressionism. Either that or his work is divided into periods to suit a particular agenda. Far from looking to unify or transform scattered texts into a coherent theory, I prefer to follow a few of their melodic and rhythmic lines, listening for what piano playing put into play—what it aroused or displaced—in the thought of Roland Barthes.

Would not flitting about theoretical discourses correspond to a kind of musical practice? Would it not correspond to a loving approach that is wary of being fitted into—bogged down by—some thesis? Barthes loved wavering; he loved the suspension of power and its territorial drive. It was the same with his status as a professor: He dreaded magisterial discourse. During his seminars, attended by an ever more numerous public, his voice would tighten with mistrust; he did not want to give a doctoral ring or kick to it. Barthes confessed that he hoped instead to create an atmosphere of hashish-smoking: "Everything is there, but *floating*." Speech frees itself from meaning and from the law. Accompanying curls of smoke and melopoeias, speech becomes more like music: *Sprechgesang* and cannabis. Barthes dreamed of himself as *Pierrot Lunaire* (Moonstruck Pierrot), who could escape what Sartre had already called the spirit of seriousness. He could thereby avoid both dogmatism and logocentrism. Barthes fluttered about from discipline to discipline: psychology of music; sociology; aesthetics; . . . and yes, even erotics. All of these approaches have value so long as we don't sink into them. When he accepted Claude Maupomé's invitation to create a radio broadcast for France Musique, Barthes evaded the roles expected of him. He was not there as a musicologist or a thinker to show his excess of soul. Instead, Barthes embraced the pleasure and arbitrariness of his tastes, intending to share them over the radio waves. He thus went about constructing his playlists like a producer who is careful to create a balance for his listeners by mixing surprise and expectation, by setting up vocal, instrumental, and symphonic tracks together. After some Dvořák, Schubert, Schumann, or Webern, he gave his listeners the "present" of listening to Maria Callas sing Bellini's *I puritani*. And then he closed his subjective "concert" with two psalms by Monteverdi, serving as a collective counterpoint to individual music. Barthes delighted in this radio play. It allowed him to construct a portrait of himself along lines he could accept: individual predilections—without learned discourse—together in fleeting complicity. For Barthes, speaking about music always came from his own emotions and his own playing, even if he never gave up the attempt to put them into some perspective.

Barthes's writings on the piano are composed of sociological insights, personal confessions, and phenomenological analyses. Differentiating himself from his initial Sartrean model, Barthes did not seek a synthesis of disciplines; he lacked such a taste for totality. At the very least, he understood that musical practices fall within the domain of sociological analysis: Piano playing is a class-based activity, and, in the nineteenth century, it was the means of discovering music. We have seen Nietzsche's insatiable appetite for musical scores, procured so he could get to know this or that piece of Schumann, or play the transcription of an opera he had heard in concert. In the absence of recording devices or sound reproductions, the piano remained the vehicle for musical exploration. On the other hand, as other means became available—like the gramophone, the radio, or even the telephone (through which Proust discovered Debussy's *Pelléas* and compulsively listened, over and over again, to Wagner's operas)—they eclipsed the use of the piano in the domestic sphere. Today it wouldn't occur to the average amateur to buy a musical score in order to get to know a piece of music when they could easily listen to it on the internet. Barthes was aware that piano playing had become a daily ritual among the bourgeoisie during the nineteenth century—a ritual that was typified by the young girl of the household who might play Chopin's waltzes for the pleasure of invited guests . . . or perhaps for the seduction of a future son-in-law for her parents. Barthes nevertheless sought to bring the piano out of these social codifications. Even if one can never fully escape them, he hoped to confound such codes. As a semiologist, he saw his wish expressed through his own piano playing. Of course a sociologist following in Bourdieu's footsteps would remind us that such a wish to escape social codes is itself part of a particular social position, just one among a range of probabilities. But this determination does not stop us from studying the displacements, or unexpected moments, that allow an individual to avoid being entirely liable for his social conditioning.

A little liberty, as Sartre suggested. . . . And Barthes exercised his own liberty by affirming the possibility of a third way for piano playing—a way to play other than through bourgeois social practices or a professional career. For Barthes also went after this other side of instrumental activity that transforms music into mere technique, as when a performer tries to wow the audience through a display of virtuosity. Barthes was disappointed by such an approach to music, preferring someone who could communicate the pleasure of playing. Rather than some cold maestro, it is better to have a pianist who may hit false notes and slip up but who gives the listener a feeling of participating in the music, or even of playing the music. Barthes mischievously blurred the distinction between professionalism and amateurism by describing his favorite players (Clara Haskil or Dinu Lipatti) as having the style of an "impeccable amateur." Instead of overly powerful performers, he praised a certain "amateur vagueness"—which is to say a fluttering due less to a lack of mastery than to a loving relation to the music. With technical mastery becoming a major criterion in conservatories and concert halls, Barthes would plead for the amateur piano as an alternative way to play. More than a pastime, the amateur piano is an ethos, a way of life. He didn't construct a reasoned demonstration to advance this type of playing, but rather began from his own tastes, maintaining that they were existential choices. Barthes was Nietzschean in his approach: It was nondialectical, self-centered, and enthusiastic. He used it to sketch out the subjective scene of his own emotions and feelings. And he extended it into a kind of practical thought used less to express some musical ineffableness than to associate it with the very pleasure it analyzes. Such pleasure is thereby refined so as to be better tasted and shared.

Through this association of the pleasure of playing with a thinking about playing, Barthes offers us more than a rehabilitation of amateurism: He suggests a phenomenology of touch at the piano. In the tradition of those philosophers who are also musicians, he conceived a mode of existence for the body in the time of music. He put the relation between thought and practice into circulation in two ways. On the one hand, his reflections on amateur playing were based on other activities like reading and painting, or on other realities like desire, touch, and affection. On the other hand, he analyzed human meanings, temporalities, and intensities all from his own experience playing the piano. Just as we saw with Nietzsche and Sartre, the most interesting thing here are the dissonances among these different orders of thought and feeling. Rather than creating a coherent and synchronous relation among tastes and ideas, the piano leads its player and its thinker to move about incessantly. Such is, without doubt, the speculative provocation of musical play: It requires changes in time and obliges the body to engage in the sonorous corporeality that is music. *To give oneself over to, to take part in, to make one's presence felt*: these are the same figures Barthes delineated in *A Lover's Discourse: Fragments*. Fickle and protean, the musician's body is led to listen, touch, and think differently according to shifting amateurisms. That is the very definition of an amateur: *l'amateur aime*, the amateur loves. Her love has none of the constancy of an obsessive. The amateur may think he is discovering and learning music, but, as Barthes suggests, he imperceptibly comes to experience himself as—and is transformed into—a body of sounds and rhythms. The amateur had certainly not imagined such possibilities, such implications, such changes! But enough suggestions. Let us now enter the scene, take a look and listen: Roland Barthes is at the piano. He opens a score.

It is Schumann again—always Schumann. The Six Concert Études on Caprices by Paganini (op. 10) are in front of him. He flips through them, reads them, and hums to himself. The second one seems doable. Unlike the first étude, the left hand here seems to have some independence, with its sixteenth note triplets and interruptions. The second étude allows the right hand to roam, taking up the measure lightly, without having to obediently follow the melody. Barthes was left-handed; he was thus attentive to that side of the body and aware of its long musical imprisonment in the role of accompaniment. It would take the actual the loss of a right arm—to wit the right arm of Paul Wittgenstein, pianist and brother of the philosopher—for a composer like Ravel to devote a concerto to the left hand. Barthes appreciated the relative independence that the Romantics, especially Chopin, had begun to give it. Nonetheless in the second part of this Schumannean étude, the two hands have to be perfectly synchronized. There is no room for fluttering about, even Romantic fluttering! And it requires rapidity: *non troppo lento*! Barthes continues to play, but at his own rhythm, or rather at his own pace. He does not respect the score's indications, preferring to slow down in order to better set up the chords. "I play the entire piece, but not to the original tempo," he confessed, evading in this way every request for him to play in public. Sometimes he stops and flips ahead a bit. The third and fourth études seem a bit difficult; he will only play a few passages from them. In the sixth, there are lots of chords, and everything depends on mood: Some days lend themselves to grand arpeggios or unfolding harmonies; others to melodic lines. It all depends. Why would one want to play a piece as one is supposed to at all costs, without allowing it to be affected by the changing psyche of the performer? Rather than as a pianist, Barthes defined himself as a "sight-reader without velocity": "I know how to read a score, but I don't know how to play." This admission reveals as much modesty as it does his avowed preference for reading. Barthes's daily piano playing consisted less in perfecting a particular piece or getting an interpretation just right than in wandering about among his collections of scores. He set up an alternative practice to technical mastery—one that, instead of perfect execution, privileged wandering, fragmentation, and sensible caprice.

Barthes didn't learn pieces by heart, because of a poor memory or perhaps his habit of using scores. He needed to read in order to play. Among the many categories of amateurs, a distinction can be made between "touchers" and "readers," which might also divide intuitive players and more intellectual players. "Touchers" touch the keyboard instinctively and call upon the memory of other pieces, joining these memories to a spontaneity in their playing. "Readers," like Barthes, read; we might imagine that he thus loved scores the way he enjoyed the "pleasure of the text." Nevertheless the analogy between these two types of reading is misleading: Reading notes does not engage the same faculties as reading words. Sight-reading is done through the eyes, but also—and above all—through the hands. This fact has considerable consequences for the empathy of a "reader" like Barthes. Without pushing the distinction too far, we can note that the incarnation implied by sight-reading a score is more intense than the imagination solicited by reading a novel. For Barthes, the pleasure of piano playing is based on joining a score to a body. He would not be able to simply "read" a score, as though he had found it in a book of music theory. "Reading" a score required sitting down to the piano and answering the call to "live" the music. For this very reason Barthes did not care much for recordings. We might be surprised that such a music lover—one who had even developed radio programs for France Musique—would not listen to albums. Nevertheless the relation that Barthes had with music was empathetic: He allowed the sound-universes that he loved to penetrate his body, while at the same time imposing his own tempo, his own feelings, and his own mistakes on the music.

Amateurs are clumsy players because of their lack of technical skill, but also because they accept a certain carelessness with regard to the exactness of their execution. Barthes had praised clumsiness elsewhere: Writing about the painter Cy Twombly, he noted the value of this blot or that smudge in his works. And even if he never wrote on the awkwardness particular to a musician, he expressed both a taste for overly slow tempos and a lack of respect for meter. Did Barthes himself play without rhythm, like Sartre did when he played a nocturne by Chopin? Giving an answer to this question requires a few qualifications about the relations each of these two habitual amateurs maintained to rhythm. Sartre was caught between his synthesist desire for synchronous immediacy and a wish to escape his own times. Barthes, less radically cleft by this contradiction, questioned the link between fixed time and subjective time, and his work took place at their juncture. He introduced syncopations or at times slowed things down, creating improbable durations. Barthes acknowledged that his tempo could be overly slow when he was confronted with the technical difficulty of certain pieces. He accepted this, relating it to a more general desire for deceleration: He hated to be rushed. For his radio interviews on France Musique or France Culture, he expressed a desire that he be able to take his time and that any silences or hesitations on his part be kept. In short, he wanted those blots or smudges of time to be preserved rather than cleaned up, as recording software would someday come to do. He wanted to preserve that lost time [*temps perdu*] that is missing from the fullness of sound produced by our efficient world.

Musical amateurism could be defined as a clumsy art that accepted its own flaws without erecting them into some anti-aesthetic. Its awkwardness would fall above or below any opposition between the intentional and the nonintentional. The amateur seeks only to find pleasure in a way of playing that provides an alternative to technical mastery. He neither performs nor completes a piece, but always begins and begins again to play it. Barthes, flipping through his scores, would thus sketch out a few interpretations. He would begin to sight-read, without necessarily going to the end. He *flirted* with the music. This is why he preferred short pieces over interminable sonatas. A longer work would require a commitment over several months—a burdensome fidelity that would not allow fleeting or random visits. With each piece, Barthes wanted to rediscover or, indeed, multiply the pleasure of beginnings. If we had to theorize such a nondefinitive approach, we could look to the writings of Blanchot on the inchoative. Or perhaps to Montaigne's *essai*, which weighs the world in such a way that one can touch without heaviness, understand with tact, circulate among references, and appropriate them according to one's own mood or caprices. Nevertheless Barthes's pleasure of reading musical scores remains at a remove from any theoretical resolution. It arises from a style, a complex of feelings, and a unique encounter between the body and the piano. Sight-reading music [*déchiffrage*] is at once close to and distinct from deciphering a text [*déchiffrement*], just as the French word *interprétation* does not have the same meaning in music ("performance") as it does in literature or philosophy ("interpretation").

Barthes's interest in the materiality of musical scores bears witness to this distinction. It was a difference that he cultivated by both bringing together and separating these two essential activities of his life: working on a text and playing the piano. Musical scores are, of course, like books, and Barthes was particularly fond of those bound editions that came down to him from generations past. Instead of buying individual scores, he played from volumes of Beethoven or Schumann in which his grandmother had indicated the fingerings when she was still a child. Books too can be passed down through family libraries and often contain annotations or underlinings that divert the modern reader's attention, leading her to dream about those thoughts left in the margins. Still, as I have already mentioned, reading music at the piano fully engages the body. Thus in the numbers he found penciled in under the measures, Barthes was able to discover the movement of past hands—a past performer's tricks to resolve technical difficulties. He placed his own fingers in the fingerings of those who preceded him, following in a more or less inflected repetition across the generations. In his *Roland Barthes by Roland Barthes*, he had noticed in his family photos the recurrence of a certain pensive position of the elbow, one that seemed passed down from father to father. No doubt Barthes thought about the bequeathing of hand positions as he played, looking at his grandmother's fingerings on the score. Such markings do not so much resemble signs as they do traces. They put the current player into a nostalgic relation to time and call upon his imagination of signs: An earlier player had been present in front of this score, and Barthes experiences with his hands the absence and presence of his grandmother. In his *Camera Lucida*, he captured the *noeme* of photography with the phrase *ça a été, that has been*: a relation to time presupposed by any printed image. In keeping with Sartre, he observed the paradox in which the imagination can make an object present without our being able to touch it. The imagination thereby creates a false perception but a true relation to the past, for the object has been there, in front of the lens. Past fingerings noted on musical scores induce a more subtle meditation on this paradox. They play on the confusion of images and signs, without anything being imposed on the mind's eye. They sketch out a past activity, a prior playing of the piano left in the grain of the page. The yellowing paper bears no visible imprint of the actual playing, but provides a trust or depository in which to leave behind prior performance as well as the time spent arranging the body's position at the piano—how to bend its fingers, move its thumbs, and flex its wrists.

Was Barthes's experience of the piano melancholic? Did his daily playing correspond to moments that were both happy and depressing at the same time—moments through which he imagined himself to be consonant with feelings now gone? We might think that his inclination for Romantic music encouraged him along these lines; his routine sight-reading became, no doubt, the *basso continuo* off of which he gave free reign to this melancholic tendency. We need not talk about any psychological illness going on here: Depression is also a necessary mode of life and one that is not incompatible with pleasure. Comparing Barthes's piano playing to that of Sartre, I notice that the latter, even if he shared a taste for Romanticism, had fun playing, even clowned around, varying his styles, moving from parody to empathy. Less eccentric, Barthes maintained a certain monotony in which he varied and modulated his feelings. Nietzsche might afford a more pertinent comparison in terms of depression, although this philosopher felt it more strongly, so pained was he by his lack of musical recognition. Still, Barthes appears more applied, less extroverted on this comparison—no doubt because he was wary of too much expressivity, of letting loose the drive of pathos.

The time Roland Barthes spent daily at the piano kept him in the present tense of habit. But he was also affected by a tendency to the past. Sight-reading allowed him to go through new pieces ad infinitum, letting him decide the amount of time he would devote to this prelude or to that intermezzo. It was a light style of reading, involving the pleasure of the surface of musical scores, punctuated by the occasional plunge, without yet sinking into musical pathos. Barthes's playing was imbued with many memories: of the composer and of previous players who had left their traces behind. But above all, more than anything, his playing was imbued with the memory of how he learned to play. Professional players progress in stages, eventually freeing themselves from their first studies. They modify their technique according to the professors who guide them at the conservatory or in master classes. The amateur, on the other hand, remains faithful to his beginnings. Even if she gets better, she never really forgets her start, such that certain deficiencies often persist—perhaps a clumsy way of holding her hands, a problem of tempo, an unequal touch, and so on. For Barthes, playing the piano brought back sedimented memories of his childhood world. He wrote a little text, "Piano-souvenir" ["Piano-memory"], in 1980, the last year of his life. In it, he evokes the nostalgia that constituted his musical playing. He explains that he never took private lessons, but instead bathed in the musicality of his family, including an aunt who gave piano lessons at Bayonne. Hearing scales played always brought this soundscape back to his mind. In an entirely Proustian manner, Barthes deployed the recollection of associated memories in order to better show that time is constituted as a past-to-come [*un passé à venir*]: "The piano was getting ready to become a memory." By introducing memory into the present time of the past, he suggested that the piano renews sound memory. What is more, in its actuality, it produces a present-as-past, a present that is colored by memory even before it becomes the past. Barthes's relation to musical practice was a factory for nostalgia beyond any act of recollection. This relation was intransitive: Ultimately it aimed less for production of memories than for a deliverance of the present from any chronology.

Like Nietzsche and Sartre, Barthes grew up without a father and associated the piano with a familial—and particularly feminine—environment. He too came out of a Protestant culture: When speaking of his interest in André Gide, he noted the writer's pianistic excellence, as well as his Reformation heritage. Nevertheless Barthes's own musical practice drew above all on a maternal religion, more than on any reference to sacred music. Although the collusion between Roland and his mother was not as exclusive as the one between the young Poulou and his mother, Barthes regularly associated the piano with the maternal bond—even if only in terms of his favorite composers. He played Schubert, he explained, for the intimist character of his music, something so foreign to the virility found in Beethoven. Barthes heard in Schubert's music a request for tenderness directed toward the mother. Schumann brought such a filial atmosphere to its height. He is the musician of the "child who has no other link than to the Mother." And here Barthes could unite his defense of amateurism with the nostalgia for his youth: Schumann was in no way amateurish, but his technique seems of the most innocent kind, without in any way imposing masculine power. His *lieder* demonstrate this with the irruption of the *Muttersprache* in their musical texts. Schumann had two women in his life: his mother, who sang, and Clara, who inspired him to such an extent that he composed a hundred lieder in their first year of marriage. At the threshold of Schumannian melancholy— which Barthes too cultivated—the maternal voice spreads out its benevolent range, far from any drive for power. Through "the" mother thus exalted in Schubert's and Schumann's music, Roland Barthes, as a pianist and insatiable sight reader, implicitly spoke of "his" mother. Her unique figure, free of any familialism, haunted his musical playing. Even her death came to resonate in Schumann's harmonies. In *Camera Lucida*, Barthes wrote about one of the last works Schumann created before he collapsed for good: "that first *Gesang der Frühe* . . . accords with both my mother's being and my grief at her death."

The sentimental landscape that Barthes associated with music certainly belongs to Romanticism: It offered him minor modes of melancholy. Sartre too, when playing Chopin, delighted in investing himself emotionally in such tonalities—going so far as to slip into a phthisic mindset. For Barthes tuberculosis was neither a metaphor nor a vicarious identification. At the age of eighteen he contracted hemoptysis, and his studies were interrupted so he could go to a sanitarium. In "The Grain of the Voice" he confides that tuberculosis is not merely an illness that hinders living but also a kind of living in itself—one that privileges interiority. During the winters he spent awaiting the return of his health, with snow falling in the Pyrenees, Barthes played Bach's preludes. He set his sadness to the rigor of *The Well-Tempered Clavier*. He found there a balance and a measure, which kept him from sinking into morbidity. He alternated between Bach and Schumann according to the needs of his emotional health. The practice of sight-reading does not preclude composition: Experiencing harmonies allows one to anticipate them and even prolong them. Any amateur can compose in the style of the composer he sight-reads regularly: One need only borrow a few melodic lines or chords and then improvise. Nietzsche never stopped dialoguing with his favorite composers in this way. And although Barthes did not have the same creative ambitions, he dreamt of composing along the lines of Schumann's intermezzi. Sometimes a melodious development arose at his fingertips, like the Divertimento in F-major (duple time) that he transcribed onto a score of two sheets as a gift to his friend Philippe Rebeyrol. Barthes also composed a small *lied* based on a poem by Charles d'Orléans; he left it open to either accompany a singer or indeed be accompanied by singing. While he did not have a taste for group music, Barthes did discover the desire to play as a duo. He composed a piece for four hands that recaptured the memory of the piano duets he had played when he was twenty years old, performing transcriptions of Beethoven's symphonies with a beloved friend. Playing as two engages a whole rhythm and art of adaptation that the side-by-side positioning of the players alone does not capture. Sartre loved the moment of merging experienced in four-handed play, whereas Nietzsche would sooner compose for two pianos. As for Barthes, he had to get used to it. He wrote that he did not like the frontal nature of concerts, preferring instead a more oblique form of listening. He did not like face-to-face encounters, and in his analyses he does not confront the objects of his study directly. He studied ideology through its myths, love through its rhetorical figures. Playing side by side with someone draws on a relation of contiguity that suited him. Both players must be heard and both must be in tune—a relation that only lasts for a time.

Despite his experience with four-handed playing, Barthes maintained a solitary practice at the piano. The company he kept with Schumann allowed him to cultivate this intimacy with the instrument. He played everyday with his mother close by, often in the afternoon before writing or going out. His avowed amateurism did not stop him from wanting to improve his technique: In 1976, for example, he took courses with Boucourechliev. He submitted himself to practicing just as he had learned to do when studying singing with Panzéra. But then he gave up on the pretext of his lectures and travels, which denied him the regularity of practice necessary to improve. In fact, he was rediscovering his particular penchant for playing the piano at his own rhythm through sight-reading and wandering across the score. Asceticism did not suit him: As he said about living in a cloister, he could appreciate solitary life in a cell so long as he was not obliged to following the tempo of others. Such dilettantism would not be terribly original if Barthes had not articulated it within his reflections on life and music. His piano playing becomes interesting for the philosophy it suggests, for the passions of taste it unleashes, and for the truth about desire it allows us to approach.

A little philosophy of piano playing crops up through the light comments Barthes made about his life with this instrument. The piano gives rise to a type of playing that led Barthes to think through, and at times theorize, diverse ideas linked to time and the body—and thus to the relation between technique and *jouissance* ["bliss" or "orgasm"]. The question was to know: whether technical constraints prevail over *jouissance*; how they might leave space for it; what other kind of *jouissance* they might give. Barthes thus came back to that well-known Nietzschean problematic of the Dionysus–Apollo paradigm. In Western culture, excess had been repressed by too much moderation [*mesure*], and only great works of art have known how to articulate order with disorder, reason with imagination, harmony with a scream. From the point of view of someone who played music, Barthes kept himself from such philosophical allegories. Instead, he asked concretely how mastery of the keyboard, which demands attention, can nevertheless authorize a certain emotional abandon. Or, more simply, how a player can guard against making false notes and at the same time find pleasure in listening to the music being played. The correctness of the touch and the exactness of the strike required impose a certain discipline on the player that is not terribly conducive to carefree listening! Those fingerings mentioned earlier, which Barthes loved to find among his old scores, reveal a certain training for the hands. Still, he sometimes attempted to ignore them in order to go directly for *jouissance*, without paying attention to technique. But all of a sudden he makes a mistake: His fingers slip, and a false note breaks his rapture. Like Orpheus, who turned back too early toward Eurydice, losing her forever, the player cannot passively abandon himself to listening. Can technique be forgotten? In this paradoxical question, Barthes glimpsed a higher degree of technique: It is only once we give ourselves totally over to it that a *jouissance*, at once active and passive, can occur.

The discovery of this *jouissance* presupposes an understanding of the relation between spontaneity and reflexivity. How can one listen to oneself play? Or how can one listen to what is being played at one's fingertips? The simultaneity of playing and listening presupposes certain accommodations: If we only want to hear ourselves, then we only play for the ear, setting up a division between the body that plays and the body that listens. The whole art of playing consists of listening to oneself *in* the act of playing, without exteriority. We can no more watch ourselves watching than hear ourselves playing. Listening is, of course, always necessary, but it requires the whole body and demands greater acuity than simply hearing. Nietzsche had understood this necessity in orienting himself toward the physiology of music. Although he took the diapason as his model to assert that we think through our ears, he also believed that listening to music depends on a particular body with its particular substantial energy. Listening thus varies from body to body. The only way to become a listener to one's own playing outside of one's own playing is to make a recording. Barthes used a tape recorder to improve his own performances in the absence of a teacher to correct or instruct him. But in *Roland Barthes by Roland Barthes*, he reveals just how much the practice of recording himself was nevertheless imbued with imagination. At the beginning, he "hears himself" [*il s'entend*], a phrase that indicates just how much he sidesteps the question of listening [*l'écoute*] and the work of analysis. Then he no longer hears himself: Only the "pure materiality" of music remains. He has the impression of having direct access to Bach or Schumann, without perceiving any work of interpretation, because it is his own interpretation: "When I listen to myself *having played*—after an initial moment of lucidity in which I perceive one by one the mistakes I have made—there occurs a kind of rare coincidence: The past of my playing coincides with the present of my listening, and in this coincidence, commentary is abolished: There remains nothing but the music." On the other hand, when he listens to recordings of other pianists, he always perceives their interpretation: He hears Richter's Bach or Horowitz's Schumann. This difference calls our attention to just how much Barthes did not seek to leave his own mark on the music he played. When he played, he created a world that had no reference other than itself: The performer fades into the background, and only Bach or Schumann remain. It goes without saying that what is at work here is a fiction of purity and immediacy. What is most important is the substantial plunge through which the pianist fades into the background, losing himself, ceasing to be a subject, and becoming entirely devoted to the sound-event and its exclusive manifestation.

The relation Barthes maintained between playing and listening to music seems to lead to the idea that no exteriority is truly possible. One cannot oneself remain at a remove from the sound-matter, as can a listener who perceives sounds. Recording oneself does not allow listening to oneself. Moreover, Barthes, just like Sartre, did not like to hear himself play, nor did he like to reread what he had written. Their rather tricky autobiographies indicate as much: The author of *The Words* pushed the autobiographical genre to parodic excess, just as the title *Roland Barthes by Roland Barthes* made its author disappear in favor of a labile and fragmentary self.

Listening to himself play had been, for Barthes, a "neutral" operation. According to his understanding of this term, such listening transformed music into an anonymous presence. We must again be clear that this presence—which, according to an old Heideggerian remnant, he called the being-there [*l'être-là*] of music—is not a definite body. Rather, listening gives proof of the metastatic nature of sound-bodies.

The ear, according to Barthes, never hears in the same way twice. It perceives new accentuations with each act of listening. In a small text from 1977 titled "Listening," he observed that music never really plays back as is: We never listen to it in the same way twice. There may be no exteriority, but there is no internal loop either. In spite of the compulsive listening by someone like Roquentin (who, in *Nausea*, listened insatiably to "Some of These Days") or by anyone else who listens over and over to a piece of music ad nauseam, Barthes wished to affirm that each listening produces a difference. Such an analysis, or idea, is certainly seductive, but does it truly correspond to our familiar experience of listening? Might it not instead depend upon a fiction that plays doubly on the unstable nature of musical matter and on the listener's faculty for avoiding repetition? Was not Barthes attempting, in some way, to justify his own magical relation to piano playing and the exclusive intimacy he felt with certain composers? The ability to escape repetition remains a major issue: It is required if we are to have any liberty or difference in our tastes and desires. Theoretical writing allows us to conceive and maintain this escape. But it also constructs a veil designed to hide a partisan, obsessive, and affective practice of listening and playing. For the opposite idea too could be maintained, namely, that repetitive listening to the same piece of music can constitute a familiar universe and create a refuge, a closed and protective accompaniment against intrusions from the outside. In exploring the nature of fascination, Barthes himself gave the example of the castrato Farinelli, who was hired by Philip V of Spain for ten or so years to sing the same tunes to him every night. This "en*chant*ment" is consonant with the seduction that music would later exert on Barthes the amateur enamored with Schumann.

Barthes's public theory of differential listening seems to legitimate, or even mask, a rather compulsive private playing. We can see another indication of this in an unpublished passage from *A Lover's Discourse: Fragments*. It concerns an example of listening dear to Barthes in which Goethe's young Werther is able to calm down by listening to Charlotte play: "It is her favorite air; and, when she plays the first note, all pain, care, and sorrow disappear from me in a moment." Barthes thinks this tune must be an old one, a shopworn melody, like the one sung daily by Farinelli. Here repetition does not produce any difference: "Soothed, distracted by an old tune, the lover is like an autistic child, skillful at reproducing musical tunes and able to spend hours listening to the same tune: perhaps because both thereby ensure that *nothing changes*." Barthes, to be sure, was not casting himself as Philip V or Werther; he could just as easily have sided with the singer, Farinelli, or the player, Charlotte. In fact, he oscillated from one side to the other, from the side of the person listening to the side of the person playing. And he listened to himself playing by switching from one role to the other: from the performer to the listener; from the lover to the loved one; from the enchanter to the enchanted. But circulating among roles like this, whether reciprocally or reflexively, functions as a closed circuit or regress *en abyme*. What is needed in order to escape the logic of the Same is a ritornello style of thinking, like that formulated by Guattari and Deleuze. Here again, the child is reassured through song. At times, perhaps while walking in the dark, a child might create different rhythms in order to escape the chaos. At other times, while doing her home-work, she might start to hum. Sometimes, after beginning a little song, he improvises on it, at risk of slipping into new territory. It is thus with the ritornello: "Along sonorous, gestural, motor lines that mark the customary path of a child and graft themselves onto or begin to bud 'lines of drift' with different loops, knots, speeds, movements, gestures, and sonorities." Just as Deleuze and Guattari did through the figure of the rhizome, Barthes developed a theory of the counterpoint and of the network. Moreover, his approach to texts as fabrics of multiple connections was also akin to a fight against models of entrenchment and filiation. Still, Barthes's idea of displacement shared more with the process of moiréing or the shifting shimmering of fabrics than it did with any hybridiza-tion of heterogeneous elements. Deleuze shared Barthes's love for Schumann, but he also liked the pop singer Claude François. And even though Barthes could at times be interested in the most trivial details of contemporary life, he kept his musical refuge separate. Was he autistic? Well, he was not schizophrenic, in any event. He did not shun the pleasure of shop-worn melodies, for, yet again, even there something perseveres that survived the graft. Barthes did not pretend to be an inventor of new ideas, preferring instead to interrogate the figures of the ordinary. Dig into an old tune, experi-ence it, and displace it: Write in order to thwart it.

Ultimately, can we not say that Barthes reveals himself more when he talks about his musical tastes than when he deploys his little philosophy of musical amateurism, however refined and se-ductive that philosophy might be? Let us, then, look to his passions. They are not too numerous. And even if there are a thousand ways to listen over and over again to a favorite composer, that choice of just one composer, or of just a few, engages the whole of a person, his mind, desires, and dreams. Elective affinities work thus: Tell me whom you listen to and I'll tell you who you are. Nietzsche accepted that all of life was a question of tastes and colors. This is why it is important to know what others listen to, or perhaps to know what that one particular other person listens to. Isn't it common for lovers and friends to ask each other what their favorite music is? Movies, food, books, and so on, are touchstones too. But music does not lend itself readily to reasoned argument. We have difficulty convincing others that a particular taste in music is well founded—short, that is, of appealing to authority. Choices are expressed with passion according to the superior intuition of some absolute community, or some radical separation from it. You like Puccini? How vulgar! Baroque music? Sure, but with which instruments? You listen to jazz? Fine, but what kind of jazz? Don't tell me that you sing *La belle de Cadix*—if so, that's where we part company. Sometimes musical disagreements can be worth breaking up over. And even if every musical taste seems acceptable, there is more going on here than cultural relativity or social branding. One's whole body, imagination, and sensitivity are required in listening, and together they set up scales of agreements and disagreements. Like Nietzsche, Barthes reveals himself through his musical choices. Sartre offered us a red herring when he gave learned interviews on music but then went back to his Chopin without telling us. Barthes too fulfilled his obligation, as an intellectual, to talk about contemporary composers. With Deleuze and Foucault, he participated in the work of the IRCAM (the Institute for Research and Coordination Acoustic/Music), which had been organized by Pierre Boulez. There Barthes discussed Ligeti, Stockhausen, Messiaen, and Carter, among others. He also commented on Webern, Boulez, and Pousseur, keeping up with the contemporary trends. Although we have no reason to doubt his sincerity, we do know that his most pertinent comments on music more often concerned classical composers.

Even if his own musical culture was broader, the constellation of composers Barthes expressed passion for was rather restricted: Mozart, Schumann, and Chopin, as well as French music from the early twentieth century. His taste for Mozart was mostly a question of mood, of *Stimmung*, as Nietzsche would have said. Barthes loved to play Mozart's Variations. Returning to the Twelve Variations on "*Ah vous dirai-je, Maman*" filled him with an unshakable happiness. Listening to Mozart's works and playing them afforded Barthes a range of light moods and feelings into which he could easily project himself. He could amuse himself with them without risk of melancholic empathy. Like most admirers [*amateurs*] of Mozart, Barthes associated his music with joy. He gave himself over to it in all innocence and was thereby able to live and think in an "A major" or "A minor" mode, depending on the occasion of whatever piece he was playing at random from a score. Mozart's music provided him magic boxes from which he composed styles for himself. Thought and habitus are thus revisited through a musical introjection of the self.

Playing music performs a particularly unique role, a role that suddenly appears here. We can become aware of it especially if we make a comparison to the imaginary projection that so occupied Barthes's writings. He always found images suspect whenever they involved processes of identification, or whenever they fixed the self into a snapshot, pose, or desire that was too obvious. In *Roland Barthes by Roland Barthes*, he fulfills, to be sure, his biographical obligations by presenting his family album. But, all the while, he constantly plays on the irony of the reflecting image. The labels he attaches to these photos mischievously inflect any pretention to construct a self-as-writer. They outstrip all attempts at interpretation, putting the photos *en abyme* by noting, for example, that here the mirror stage is at work, or there a family romance is at play. In *Camera Lucida*, Barthes describes the effect photographs had on him by referring to stings, holes, stains, and cuts. Images seem thus to infiltrate the body in order to make it suffer. But this irruption happens by surprise, unbeknownst to the viewer. It enters into a uniquely centrifugal relation to the self, transporting the self beyond itself. On the other hand, an introjection by sound presupposes a consensual, quasi-fusional incorporation. In a recovery of Nietzsche's physiology of music, Barthes avoided both narcissism and imagined abandonment. Instead, he fashioned a labile self in a mode of sound. By taking in certain rhythms and harmonies, he lived his own subjectivity in the joyous becoming of the music he loved. He did not, of course, have any original ideas about Mozart's music to write about—apart, that is, from the emotions that Mozart's compositions aroused in him. And this effect, shared by any number of amateurs, is of interest to us most of all for how it brings to light a musical way of living and thinking. It suggests a way for the self to experience itself as music.

Barthes's greatest musicological concern comes down essentially to the preference that had to be given either to Schumann or to Chopin. He struggled retrospectively with Nietzsche on this question of taste, which engages a whole style and a whole world. It is extremely important to discern what is at stake in this confrontation, as well as what the existential meaning—at once personal and philosophical—of Barthes's preference for Schumann was. There is nothing obvious that would oppose these two composers, especially given that they shared a mutual admiration. The binary generated is even more surprising because we know that Barthes was resistant to this type of paradigm that forces an either-or choice:

He felt it was like blackmail. In fact, however, the choice between the two developed little by little from an ambivalence Barthes felt in regards to Chopin. Spread out across some rather scattered reflections, we can see that Barthes appreciated Chopin differently, depending on whether he was analyzing, listening to, or playing his music. First, he sorted out Chopin's works, denigrated his concertos and his waltzes for different reasons. As a rule, he preferred shorter forms over the concerto. But such a personal taste, which he expressed in the phrases "I like (or love)" [*j'aime*] or "I don't like" [*je n'aime pas*], does not justify an argument—it remains a weak basis on which to denigrate Chopin. If the concertos could be criticized, it was for having given an almost exclusive place to the piano, leaving the orchestra in the position of accompaniment. Barthes did not like the waltzes either, even though they are short forms. Here he agreed with Nietzsche, who had pointed out a side to Chopin that was sometimes too French, too drawn to high society. Barthes found the waltzes to be overly sophisticated and excessively inclined toward virtuosity. On the other hand, he appreciated the mazurkas. Again he agreed with Nietzsche, although their preference was not based on the same criteria. Nietzsche, the great admirer of Chopin, considered him to be the genius of melody. Barthes appreciated instead his tonal indetermination. In the mazurkas he found an art of modulation, which he attributed less to dissonance than to the effects of a "tonal moiré." Nietzsche came back to forms that clearly distinguished song from melody, and this return must assuredly have been of vital importance after the Schumann of his youth and—above all—after his admiration for Wagner. For his part, Barthes felt a certain reserve about forms that were too distinct and had an obvious melodic line. Instead he appreciated those works of Chopin that blurred this distinction, notably through their use of the left hand. Chopin had often accorded it a certain independence, and even, sometimes, supremacy. Along these same lines, Barthes gave himself over to a rather wild psychoanalytic interpretation of Chopin's first prelude, noticing a drive that was being stifled under its melody. "A mobile swelling of the entire musical substance comes from the separated body of the child, of the lover, of the lost subject. . . . Something swells, does not yet sing, aspires to utter itself, and then disappears." This time introjection gives way to projection as Barthes appropriates a malleable Chopin for himself. Sound-matter becomes able to receive the states of the soul when its listener is desperately in love.

The permeable nature of Chopin's music gives its pianistic interpretation a great deal of freedom. Barthes's distancing of himself from it can be seen as a concern to protect himself. He resisted letting himself be impressed by the style of other performers, inasmuch as their music would tug at his sensitive nerves or touch upon his deep feelings. In such resistance to listening to others, we can see one of Barthes's little personal mythologies at work: namely, that the pure materiality of music would require the erasure of any performative aspect to it. The touchstone of Chopin's technique on which such a defiance could take hold was the *tempo rubato*. This small discrepancy between the left and right hands gives a rhythmic effect to the melody, allowing very diverse styles to be imprinted on the music. Abusing *rubato* can lead to vulgarity; good performers have to discover its art of proportion. Among them, Arthur Rubinstein made it into a unique refinement definitive of his style. And this is what displeased Barthes. So utterly resistant to listening to performances that were too unique, he could not stand the *rubato* of others. He thus complained, for example, about Richter's *rubato* because it did not correspond to his own internal rhythm. Barthes attributed his discomfort to Chopin's music itself, because it emphasizes details and solicits affected playing. Instead of overly precious performances, Barthes championed a disinterested impregnation by the amateur's music who "establishes himself *graciously* (for nothing) in the signifier: in the immediately definitive substance of music, of painting; his praxis, usually, involves no *rubato* (that theft of the object for the sake of the attribute)." Barthes's critique of sophistication did not arise simply from a disagreement over the performances of others. It also resulted from his own pianistic limits. Chopin's music requires a virtuosity that he didn't think himself capable of, or at least that he had no desire to acquire, ever careful as he was to maintain his amateurism. Barthes's musical taste was thus also determined by the limits of his own playing. He confessed to the difficulty Chopin presented: The left hand often seemed too difficult. He therefore kept himself to just a few preludes. On the other hand, listening to Schumann, he felt the desire to play—precisely because he could play!

Barthes regularly expressed his love for Schumann. It was as though he was making a private declaration trimmed with musicological commentaries. Little by little, in secret, he constructed theoretical oppositions with which he could engage Nietzsche in an argument. But it was in a spirit of merger that Barthes, during a radio broadcast that he had devoted to Schumann, said it most simply: "I love Schumann." [*J'aime Schumann*.] He confessed to finding an absolute satisfaction in Schumann's music that went beyond the pleasure of listening. In his *A Lover's Discourse: Fragments*, Barthes defined this fulfillment as "a perfect and virtually eternal success" of an imaginary assumption: "I adhere to the image, our proportions are the same: exactitude, accuracy, music." Schumann satisfied him—but what does that mean exactly? To understand, we have to go back to the meaning of "loving Schumann" and how it differs from the paradigm "I like / I don't like." At face value, this declaration functions as a distinction. By declaring this passion,

Barthes imposes his choice on others, obligating them to situate themselves in relation to it. His choice carries with it a subtext, just as we might find in a novel by Françoise Sagan: "And you, do you like Schumann?" Oddly, however, when Barthes drew up a list of his likes and dislikes in *Roland Barthes by Roland Barthes*, Schumann was not on it. Yet references to music dominate this rather surreal inventory, which juxtaposes ice-cold beer, watches, peonies, Sartre, and the Marx Brothers. His list of likes singles out Gould, Handel, the piano, and all Romantic music. His dislikes include the harpsichord, Rubinstein, Satie, Bartók, Vivaldi, children's choirs, Chopin's concertos, Burgundian branles, Renaissance dance tunes, the organ, and Marc-Antoine Charpentier, with his trumpets and kettle drums. Barthes insisted on making clear that these expressions of taste went beyond any game of self-portraiture according to one's own whim. They engage a mode of corporeal being: "Hence, in this anarchic foam of tastes and distastes, a kind of listless blur gradually appears in the figure of a bodily enigma, requiring complicity or irritation." Because we know that Schumann was Barthes's favorite composer, his absence from Barthes's list indicates that he exceeded any affirmation of taste. Schumann engaged something beyond pleasure, and even beyond *jouissance*. His music could fulfill Barthes by allowing his entire body to identify with its rhythms and harmonies. Schumann would be found missing from any bouquet of Barthes's tastes because he is the quintessence of music, which is to say that, for Barthes, he was the quintessence of life as music.

Barthes went further still: "The true Schumannian pianist—*c'est moi*." This was less a claim of some technical supremacy than an expression of empathy from an admirer [*amateur*]. Any player might be tempted to claim that he alone is able to understand the musical creator he admires so passionately, that he is the only one who truly knows how to play the composer. Such passions can lead to abuses of authority, but they can also reveal an understanding beyond all knowledge. We see this at work in Patrice Chéreau, who, after having watched others direct the plays of Koltès, declared that he would take them up again himself and restore a sense of seriousness. Barthes knew *his* Schumann better than any other performer. But the appropriation he made of this composer was not based on knowledge. Instead, it revealed his perfect and unmediated accord with Schumann's music. Such an appropriation meant that the internal truth of the Schumannian piano became absolutely incarnated in the body of the one who played it with so much love. He tried in vain to attribute this sublime empathy to Schumann's music itself, for Barthes was above all expressing his own relation to piano playing. Although he claims that Schumann's music is, through some intrinsic quality, made for being played rather than listened to, his arguments can be reduced to saying that this music involves the body that plays it. As such, they can be applied to any number of other Romantic composers, like Chopin or Liszt, even if their works call for different types of touch and different feelings. "Loving Schumann" is thus a declaration through which Barthes exposes his own body as a pianist.

Barthes's admiration for Schumann took a more theoretical turn when he began to construct scales of value and aesthetic and political oppositions. In a preface to a book on Schumann by Marcel Beaufils, Barthes sang the praises of the piano and set the instrument into an ideological context. This little text dates from 1979, and the semiotic-Marxist analyses of his *Mythologies* were far behind him. Nevertheless, in this text Barthes sketched out a historical and social perspective based on playing and listening to the piano. By defending Schumann, who had become the victim of disdainful neglect, Barthes sought to rehabilitate interiority, intimacy, and uniqueness against the "presumptions of the universal": "The individual has become increasingly gregarious; he wants collective, massive, often paroxysmal music, the expression of *us* rather than of *me*." Barthes's criticism updated Nietzsche's reproaches of Wagner and of Wagnerism. Barthes too expressed a reticence at the total spectacle that saturated opera and held back individuality by drowning out instrumental divisions. Faced with such vulgarization, Barthes wanted to make the piano a sphere of resistance against the music industry and the monopoly of technique. According to Barthes, recording music onto albums had deprived instrumental music of its flesh and feeling. The only way to compensate for this loss had become an excess of performance. Through technical virtuosity or an excess of sound, affected music achieved a success that devalued the essentially private Schumannian piano. Barthes thus presented Schumannian forms—intermezzi, Albumblätter, Kreisleriana, and so on—as unique objects that could be opposed to the great organ of mass-music. He was thus led to construct a series of implicit oppositions: brevity / length; lightness / heaviness; fragmentary / total; divided / unified; nostalgia / presentism; solitude / mass. These oppositions allowed him to transform his taste for Schumann into an aesthetics of desire: "Loving Schumann, doing so in a certain fashion *against* the age . . . can only be a responsible way of loving: it inevitably leads the subject who does so and says so to posit himself in his time according to the injunctions of his desire and not according to those of his sociality."

Lightness, fragmentation, dissent: Barthes's Schumannian values are rather close to Nietzsche's artistic philosophy. And yet. . . . And yet we have seen how the philosopher-musician Nietzsche violently renounced Schumann, his childhood love. Barthes did not recapitulate this relationship; he was unable to allow such malice toward his beloved composer. But he forgets that Nietzsche had wanted to "liquidate" Schumann and Romanticism by constructing a genealogical descent that would go from the great European style of Mozart, through the transition of Beethoven, to the new era incarnated by Wagner. Having to destroy his own idols, Nietzsche came to confuse Schumann and Wagner. The sacrifice was necessary for his own personal salvation, even if it meant lumping the two together in a denunciation of Romanticism and decadent modernity. Still, Barthes did pause at some of Nietzsche's more savage pages, and he ruminated on them as though experiencing a personal injury. In the radiobroadcast he devoted to Schumann, Barthes wished to exorcise the evil spirit attached to Nietzsche's cruelty. To the opening question by Claude Maupomé—"How do you listen to him?"—Barthes responded in a rather touching manner, declaring:

I listen to him as I love him. So perhaps you will ask: "How do you love him?" Well there, I am unable to answer, for I would say that I love him precisely with that part of me which remains unknown to me. I know that I have always loved Schumann, and I have always been sensitive to the fact that—as always when you love someone—I feel like he isn't being loved like he should be, that he has never been loved enough, and I am thinking in particular about a moment from the last century, the execution of someone I love, namely Schumann, by someone I admire, namely Nietzsche.

His defense of Schumann thus unfolds as a request for amorous redress. Rather than arguing with Nietzsche, Barthes sought to disarm the Nietzschean attack by moving it to a psychological playing field. He deliberately incriminates a few lines from the most scathing text Nietzsche wrote against Schumann in *Beyond Good and Evil*. Nietzsche had already broken with German culture and was wandering along the shores of the Mediterranean. There he expressed his relief that a Romanticism like Schumann's had come to an end. He relegated it to a jingoistic music that resonated with no great European idea. Schumann was thus unlike Beethoven, who had been able to make his music resonate with Rousseau, the Revolution, Schiller, Shelley, and Byron. Nietzsche's criticisms must have hurt Barthes all the more because they also touched upon his particular sensitivity. Indeed, they could have been addressing him directly: "Schumann with his taste, which is fundamentally a *small* taste (being a dangerous tendency towards calm lyricism and a drunkenness of feeling, which is twice as dangerous among Germans), going constantly to the side, timidly excusing himself and retreating, a noble, tender creature, who reveled in nothing but anonymous happiness and pain, a type of little girl and *noli me tangere* from the start: This Schumann was already a merely *German* event in music."

Against these attacks, Barthes pleaded his case on three fronts. First, he turned the accusation around by showing that the so-called pusillanimity of the composer was in fact a strength, a nobility. Barthes thereby linked Schumann to Nietzsche's aristocratism. He then underlined the presence of a certain barbarity in Schumann's treatment of musical themes. The apparent simplicity of Schumann's forms demonstrated an art that knew how to unite the Dionysian and the Apollonian. Barthes adopted a subtle psychological point of view in order to compare Nietzsche and Schumann, to the benefit of the latter. His comparison considered the serious question of the illness that affected both creative spirits, who ultimately sank into that same dark night of madness. Nietzsche's madness fell under mythomania and paranoia, whereas Schumann was manic-depressive and melancholic. His madness tended toward melancholia and anorexia. The criteria for such diagnoses rest on the different theatricality and intensity of their insanities.

By observing that Schumann refused the "glorious mask" of insanity, Barthes kept his distance from the grand declarations made by a Nietzsche who was transformed into the Antichrist, Dionysus, and Zarathustra. Barthes did not conflate the two insanities. He sketched out instead the picture of a nocturnal psyche that would link Schumann to Werther, Novalis, and Heine. The melancholy incarnated by the song of his *Mondnacht* (Moonlit Night, part of Op. 39, *Liederkreis*) would be quite removed from any hysterical fits of orgiastic madness. And instead of the coupling of Apollo and Dionysus, Barthes preferred that of Florestan and Eusebius. Schumann had identified himself with them; he used the name of one, and then the other, as his own signature, and joined the two in his *Carnaval*. This play of masks allowed Schumann to couple courage with dreaming, the masculine with the feminine, conflict with fusion. Barthes observed that Schumann's music united simplicity and ethical nobility—and noted in passing that such a combination was absent in Bizet's work.

This little jab at Nietzsche's tastes indicates the third front of Barthes plea: a competition among composers. Barthes held Schumann up as a touchstone in the history of music and thereby contested Nietzsche's decadentist version. Affirming Schumann's excellence opens up possible critiques of Beethoven for having confused the piano with an orchestra, or Wagner for his "comic flares." But Barthes took his greatest revenge in comparing Schumann to Chopin, Nietzsche's favorite composer. His somewhat artificial opposition between them becomes clearer in light of this revenge by proxy. According to Barthes, Chopin's music sins in its excess of sophistication and virtuosity. It pays exclusive attention to melody, whereas Schumann never forgot the equal importance of rhythm. Was this a petty and German affair, as Nietzsche had said? Barthes sought to extricate Schumann from questions of historical time or nationality. Schumann is fundamentally "out-of-date" [*inactuel*] and "non-territorial"—a claim Deleuze and Guattari take up in their *Thousand Plateaus* when they affirm that Schumann's music "deterritorializes the refrain [*ritornello*]."

Barthes seems to suggest that the music we love knows no country. The subject who is in love has only one home, only one attachment: the person he loves. This nomadism creates new cartographies, beyond established musical frontiers. Barthes was thus able to associate Schumann with Fauré, Debussy, and Ravel. (The label given to this other musical tradition that Barthes liked—"French music"—was more a way to refer collectively to these composers than any genuine national identity.) He learned to love Fauré through his melodies, notably *La lune blanche*, thanks to the singer Panzéra, with his not terribly "lyrical" pronunciation. He appreciated Debussy in his *Pelléas et Mélisande*, finding there both the atmosphere of a forest at night and a nonlyrical melody.

And finally Ravel—indeed, Ravel above all, for so many reasons that remain difficult to explain. There was Barthes's geographical proximity to this composer, whose origins lay in the Pays Basque. And there was also his so-called French quality, which he took from Couperin and that touched the deepest part of Barthes's taste for a composer who could exhaust forms from within, without having recourse to avant-gardist outbursts. Barthes played Ravel's Sonatine and composed in his style. Indeed, he composed more in Ravel's style than he did in Schumann's, just as Sartre took his inspiration more from Debussy than from Chopin. Ravel is more than a touchstone: He is a point of intensity that reveals a sensibility and a taste for combination. He has a sense of play that unites audacity and modesty. Barthes was able to recognize this exceptionality; he did not give in to the persistent cliché of Ravel the neoclassicist who merely adapted older forms. The dissenting force of Ravel's music has long been underappreciated: since at least Satie's nasty quip—"Ravel refuses the *Légion d'honneur*, but his music accepts it"—and right through to a certain progressive doxa that glorifies Debussy's innovating spacings to the detriment of Ravelian devices. It would require the independent spirit of someone like Jankélévitch, who was a philosopher-musicologist as well as a pianist, to show the daring of Ravel's moves. Confounding the petty national mythology of French measure and mannerism, Jankélévitch wrote: "The music of Ravel proves that France is the country not of moderation but of passionate extremism and acute paradox. It is a question of testing how far the mind can go in any given direction, of taking without any weakening all the possible consequences of certain attitudes. The result is adventure, scandal, and the abandonment of prejudices; we are led to this point by the passionate, bold French imagination, which is not afraid of going to the extreme limits of its power."

In playing Ravel, Barthes found a common sensibility, a restrained radicality, an acute awareness of older forms. We might imagine that he discovered a modernity other than that of the avant-garde, for he "played" Ravel—and not Bizet—against Wagner. As for any other aesthetic rupture, Barthes knew how to avoid grand discourses on the progress of new music. Far removed from the main musicological and philosophical currents of his day, Jankélévitch too, though for different reasons, put forth Ravel (as well as several Spanish composers, from Albéniz to Mompou) against a triumphant Germanism, in the same way that he preferred reading Baltasar Gracián to reading Heidegger. Barthes's taste for Ravel avoided such nationalist stakes. But it also testifies to his own out-of-place uniqueness. Like the misidentified "classical" composer, Barthes had a lucid relation to modernity: He engaged its ruptures without succumbing to the traps of a *tabula rasa*. Barthes and Ravel shared certain moves: They would leave behind, or rather exhaust, models instead of destroying them. Each, in their own way, moved among forms, questioned them, and displaced them. In doing so, they finished them—in the sense of both finishing them (putting the final touches on them) and finishing them off (deposing them). Ravel enjoyed trying everything: waltzes, minuets, sonatas, concertos, ballets. He composed intense tombeaux without recourse to the great organ associated with the sublime. Could we not say that Barthes too wandered among references and genres? He could be Sartrean, Brechtian, or Lacanian; he would read Chateaubriand or Sollers; he analyzed myths, the theater, fashion, the novel, photography, the language of love; in his analyses, he parodied scholarly and philosophical treatises; he avoided autobiographical traps, all the while talking about himself. Many an academic judge has seen all of this as nothing more than an *auberge espagnole*, the kind of place where you find only what you yourself have brought. They get lost in Barthes's fluttering about. They lose sight of just how much Barthes hijacked, confounded, and exhausted the objects and discourses he devoted himself to every time he did so. He thereby invented his own uniqueness through them without nullifying them.

Barthes is always off to the side of the place where we expected him to be. For just such reasons, Ravel was certainly the musician who most corresponded to him—more than Schumann, for whom he saved his affection. But could one say, "I love Ravel" just as one says, "I love Schumann"? Such a declaration would acquire a schmaltzy taste in regard to what such a name as Ravel endorses: a felicitous lucidity of feeling and an absolute intensity of artifice. More than affinities do, one's preference for a particular composer engages a whole complex of sensations, passions, and sexuality. The emotion that causes one to breathe faster and brings tears to the eyes reveals the very corporeality of musical playing—assuming that the body is not reduced to sense impressions. This emotion mobilizes both the imagination and thought. Piano playing calls upon the performer's entire body: the eyes and ears, but also the heart, the lungs, and the genitals. Barthes's testimonials about his own playing sketch out a discreet phenomenology of piano playing—perhaps more interesting to us than his explicit reflections on musical amateurism. His descriptions allow us to approach the nature of touch more closely, as well as the question of what rhythm produces in the body and how it can accentuate *jouissance*. We see this in his account of contact with the keyboard. In one of his last texts, published in the journal *Panorama de la musique*, Barthes explained that the ivory keys [*les touches*] play a large role in his pleasure and involvement with the piece being played. The touch is at once "soft and firm," because the keyboard is smooth but not slippery. Rather than revisit the distinctions Sartre made concerning the ontology of the slippery and the rough, Barthes limited himself to observing that such contact owes less to a light touch than to "a sensual dialogue between the ivory shelf and the cushion of skin." To be sure, he went back to his love for language in order to explain that the verb "to play" in Spanish is *tocar*, "to touch" [*toucher*], which indicates a corporeal activity. Nevertheless, his remarks on the complex sensation produced by the hand on the keys suggest a tactile phenomenology.

This way of thinking through the pianistic touch allows us to understand how hearing passes through the musculature and bending of the fingers. It also reveals the chiasmic effects that both Sartre and Merleau-Ponty described: By touching the keys, the performer is in turn touched. Although he does not, of course, receive the intention of another body, he nevertheless unleashes a sound that then enters him. The pianist is at once touching and touched according to a subtle confusion between tactile touching and emotional touching—a confusion that allows us to say in two ways that we are "touched" by the piano. Barthes suggests; he does not press. Still, he went far in his investigation of this unique corporeality, especially when it raised the question of pleasure. Piano playing requires mastery and submission at the same time: One has to master the instrument, possess the keys, and impose a fingering on them; but to take pleasure in playing, one has to submit to the piano's mechanics and to learning a piece of music. The desire for *jouissance* gets hammered out through a combination of constraints and impulses. Barthes picked out the motif and figure for this process: the strike [*le coup*]. The word *coup* in French designates both the rhythmic beating of the keys and the impact thus produced.

Sartre was sensitive to melody; Nietzsche, to timbre. Barthes was most sensitive to rhythm. He was particularly interested in the beat, and his approach to the classical repertory seems to come from a conception of rhythm that belonged more to contemporary music. In this respect, he remarked how the indications of movement had been flattened out by the Italian system of dynamics that, starting in the eighteenth century, reduced them to the velocity of the measure. Taking the term *movement* in the sense of a theatrical engagement, Barthes saw here the opening of a corporeal scene: The body is engaged to move, to vibrate, to perform as a musical organism. He balked at following this *presto* or that *agitato*, because, according to him, true movement depended on the rhythm, and, more fundamentally, on the beat. When writing about Schumann's *Davidsbündlertänze* or *Fantasiestücke*, he emphasized the shocks produced by the short themes to the detriment of the harmonic development. More than a musicological argument, he was defending a performance appropriate to his own style, which is to say his own way of feeling the music through his body. Barthes liked strong, obsessive rhythms; he liked accents, syncopations, and off-beat rhythms. These beats become heartbeats, giving rhythm to the irrigation of the player's muscles. Music is "what beats in the body, what beats the body, or better: [. . .] this body that beats." Barthes had analyzed at length the imagery of blood in the works of Michelet. He linked it to Michelet's conception of History as nourished by a clash of depleted or redemptive bloods. This apoplexy—both a hemorrhaging and an intense emotion [*coup de sang*]—mobilizes people and distributes on-beats into the fabric of individual and collective bodies. The description Barthes gave to the body at the piano rediscovers this energy of a sanguine rhythm, which brings together the flow and the strike.

Sanguine euphoria and sensual touch set the piano into an erotic scene. The player's body displays the movements and symptoms of this scene. The independence of the hands allows us to distinguish between the two different registers that Barthes named the beat and the caress. The left hand makes the strike heard in the brutality of the rhythm, while the right hand follows the movement closely. This Schumannian division reveals fantastical representations of the body and its divided eroticism: The right side, with its soft and linear touch, is reserved for pleasure, whereas the left side aims for *jouissance*. Barthes described the jolts of the left hand thus: "it pricks, it knocks"; "it rises, it extends"; "it showers, it comes undone"; "it strikes, it beats"; "it dances, but it also begins snarling all over again, beatings." Instead of breaking in the body by learning piano technique, Barthes wished to see the "beat's ecstatic recurrence" [*le retour jouissif du coup*]: "What is required is that *it beat* inside the body, against the temple, in the sex, in the belly, against the skin from inside." This erotic dimension is distinct from the Romantic approach, which was supposed to express the states of the soul—its joy or sadness. But the strike is not expressive, and when Barthes put forward *accent* as the true nature of music, he took care to specify that it neither meant nor represented any emotion whatsoever. Accent is a beating that makes manifest the organic life of the musician's body through its strikes. Here we can no doubt see the originality of Barthes's comments on piano playing: Despite his taste for asocial and melancholic pleasure and beyond his praise for amateur dandyism, it was *jouissance* that he sought and attempted to represent by the "strike"—both the one given and the one received. "The body must pound," he wrote, even though the pianist delicately caresses the keys. To pound, to be pounded, to become tense, to relax—pianistic movements are eminently sexual.

Piano playing comes close to onanism. It was in this way that Barthes described the ascending pleasure he felt in playing. He experienced a progressive sexual tension—at once passive and active—which came about according to his rhythms. In speaking about the third *Kreisleriana*, he stressed its pitched pace that was "lifted up, stretched out, erected." Through a certain empathy, his writings stress these terms of movement, which come to represent: erection, back-and-forth movements, momentary droopings followed by the return of stiffness to the body that curls into itself and then explodes. The piece enters and leaves; it provokes secretion, swallowing, or revulsion. By distinguishing the German word *Rasch* from the otherwise equivalent Italian term *presto*, Barthes overinterpreted this performative indication to a particular end. He wanted to discover in *Rasch* the sexual power of the desire that nimbly leads both pianist and listener toward an unknown, disseminated *jouissance*. This indication guides him, owing to the musical requirements of the piece as written. But it does not hold out the prospect of some object that would fulfill his desire. Such conduction happens "as if I had a limb swept away, *torn off* by the wind, whipped toward a site of dispersion which is precise but unknown." In another text, Barthes described the breathlessness, haste, anxiety, and building to orgasm provoked by a music that penetrates one's muscles and guts. We begin to understand his impulsive investment in music—a side of him that was less smooth than his championed amateurism. Through his commentaries, which go beyond metaphor, Barthes wrote not only a lover's discourse, but also an erotics based on his own desire. When he promoted the pleasures of beginnings and interruptions, of the attack and the strike, of caressing and stretching out, he appropriated musical dilettantism in order to invest it with a solitary and polymorphous sexuality. Through reciprocal stimulation, the musical piece brings about the *jouissance* of the player, who embodies it with his own desire. This erotics is nevertheless unlike a lover's discourse, for it does not enter into a particular vocabulary of figures. Instead it remains indeterminate to the point that its subject cannot refer to it except sporadically through the use of an undefined pronoun: *It* pounds; *it* escapes capture. All of his commentaries on the playing of music form a metonymy of this desire that has no image: Barthes observed that when he played, "Something gets a hard-on."

This erotics of the piano gives voice to the musician's body, to his impulses and beats. It also signals the impotence of language to say just what is at play in such desire. And here we probably see the principal stakes of Barthes's piano playing, beyond any pleasure he felt describing his musical tastes or amateur activities. There are no figures that could give an account of the impulsive life of the pianist: Semiology and psychoanalysis alike stumble over such a network of sensations, feelings, and imaginings. Barthes's emphasis on the piano player's body—a body that is mixed together with the musical materiality in a flowing reciprocity—highlights a discrepancy in his work, for he never approached music in the same way he did myths, literature, Japan, fashion, or love. It remained impossible for him to isolate any structure or code that would have expelled his own involvement from the experience of the piano. Barthes's last writings, of course, also witness a relinquishing of semiotics in favor of an avowed subjectivity; we can see this in the autobiography that played out in the obituary he wrote about photography.

The touch of the piano accompanied Barthes throughout his life. From the very beginning, he experienced the unrepresentable nature of music and the way playing music substantially implicates both the self and the body. He came to feel, therefore, that knowledge or external discourses were somehow inappropriate. Yet, for all that, Barthes did not fall back on the mysteries of ineffability. He loathed such mysteries and sought to demythologize them in the domain of literature. The little mythologies that surround the Romantic poet or artist associate him with false profundities. Barthes, on the other hand, had both the audacity and lightness to speak about his own love and desire for piano playing. His writings on music sketch out an escape from learned discourses—even if he always wanted (and knew how) to unite knowledge and taste [*le savoir et la saveur*], as he declared in his inaugural lecture at the *Collège de France*.

Barthes's insistence on the body of the musician overthrows the imperialism of semiology, of which he indeed had become the entitled authority. Two years before this consecration at the *Collège de France*, he had revealed himself, as ever, through his listening to Schumann, writing: "I actually hear no note, no theme, no contour, no grammar, no meaning, nothing which would permit me to reconstruct an intelligible structure of the work." This refusal to hear or read a structure in the music indicates a clear mistrust of codes and a care to preserve a substantial and polymorphous listening. Jankélévitch, in his *The Je-ne-sais-quoi and the Almost-Nothing* [*Le je-ne-sais-quoi et le presque-rien*], also observed the insufficiency of a grammar to account for the phenomenon of music: "Innumerable glosses and interminable commentaries would not exhaust the charm of music, or exhaust it, so to speak, at the limit. Inextricable complex and unfathomable mystery, this elusive charm is at once profound and superficial: profound because the player can never have finished unfolding its inexhaustible riches; superficial because it remains entirely within the indivisible phenomenality of its perceivable style. . . ." By refusing any structural decrypting of music and any allegation of its unspeakable mystery, Barthes attempted to approach this phenomenon in a different way. Musical semiology did not interest him; he preferred instead to describe the sonorous transformations of his own body in order to approach a different truth about music. He did not put his personal impressions up to a formal analysis. Instead, he expressed humbly—yet with force—a corporeal dimension to music that had been ignored or neglected by semiologists and musicologists. He observed that the way music escapes any code is particularly manifest in the style we call *parlando*. We can apply this term beyond singing, to include any instrument that bears a unique voice [*parole*]. Such musicality breaks free of any linguistics; speech acts become absorbed by a body language that exceeds signs: "The instrument (the piano) speaks without saying anything, in the fashion of a mute who reveals on his face the inarticulate power of speech [*parole*]." Music does not create signs, but it is spoken through bodies. These bodies join with it, trouble it, and bring it into existence in a multiplicity of unstable forms that are only approachable through metaphor. Music is a "continuous *big bang*." Semiology must step aside in order to give way to this chaos. Even though it is unreadable, this chaos inheres even in the most seemingly harmonious music.

The greatest surprise we find in Barthes the pianist now comes into view: This most refined and sharpest analyst of sign-systems loved music precisely because it freed him from codes and discourses. Rather than being attracted to the structures of music, he gave himself over to passions without language when playing the piano. He sought the imaginary excess of the body more than any measurement of sound-spaces. His passions did not require any theatricality or grand declarations in the style of Artaud about the deposition of the Word or the subversion of the organless body. These passions arise in our ordinary lives of shared feelings and imaginations. They arise whenever discourses become heavy and inappropriate—when music constitutes a refuge as well as a desert. In an unpublished text from *A Lover's Discourse: Fragments*, Barthes recounts a little scene in which he had to suffer through a social call that utterly bored him. Fortunately, the radio was playing a Beethoven trio, and he was thus able to extricate himself from the chatter. This banal situation almost becomes a figure that traces his relation to music: Seized by a feeling of unreality, Barthes feels happy because he is intact and impermeable to social chattering. He drew this conclusion: "Music never says anything; it doesn't burden me with any discourse; it does not seek to replace my discomfort with anything (which would be the best way to aggravate it); it suspends it: it is an *epoche*, something like the degree zero of all systems of meaning, those systems that are indiscreetly busy repressing in me the only freedom I care about today:

the freedom to be delirious (*mainomai*: I am lost, I am in love)." Whether love-craze, bacchic frenzy, elation, or escape: through music, the suspension of language opens up to the most unbridled intimate excesses. Nevertheless, music does not constitute another world, as would, say, a psychotic delirium. Music allows us to follow our own course willingly. We can defer [*différer*] the tempo of discourses and let go of the grammar of the powers that be.

Barthes's musical playing revealed a passion that goes against the theoretical lines of his own work. It nevertheless did not compose a contretemps, an off-beat, as it had for Sartre, who thereby escaped from synchronicity with his own times. It also did not constitute some elementary or primordial life, like the one underlying all of Nietzsche's ambitions. Rather, his playing presents itself as a velocity, a pace that allowed its subject to go at his own rhythm and follow his own personal speeds and movements. In one of his last seminars, "How to Live Together," Barthes proposed a notion that allows us to define such a detachment: the idiorhythm. His specific inspiration here was the monastic life in the Béguinages that defined a social utopia according to a use of time that was at once singular and collective. The ethical and political stakes of such an organization must allow each person to follow a personal rhythm, all the while remaining integrated into one community. More generally, this aspiration, or perhaps fantasy, gave rise to the possibility of stepping to one's own beat and escaping any imposed cadence—whether the cadence be that of the mother, whose pace the child is made to follow despite his small limbs; or that of power, which imposes biorhythms in order to keep the bodies of society in line. Playing music was no doubt an idiorhythm for Barthes, and his defense of amateurism falls under this purview as well: Do not follow an imposed rhythm; do not regulate yourself according to a metronome; instead, allow yourself to connect the impulse of your body to the movement of the score. Playing Schumann was certainly one way to remain off to the side of contemporary hype. Even if Barthes knew how to stay informed about all the modernities and avant-gardes of his own time, he also kept a distance from them, maintaining his ability to veer off and not blindly follow the trends. Music was his step to the side.

Washington Square Village, Fall 2007

Five

RESONANCES

When they sat down to the piano, did they merely play the piano? By following Nietzsche, Sartre, and Barthes in their regular practice of this instrument, we discover just how much playing music carries with it a whole life of feelings, a life that extends into our social and intellectual activities. This initial intuition leads us, through the touch of these three thinkers, to the metonymic power of the piano. Although often reserved for moments of solitary intimacy, piano playing does not leave the rest of one's days intact. Even without constructing a theory for it, each of these three testified to a kind of displacement that allows us to think, love, and dream in music—or, inversely, that allows us to play music by giving our whole body over to it. By putting ourselves into their fingerings we can discover the *musical* body—and not just the *musician's* body—of these players. We can thereby approach their existences that were at once autonomous and yet tied to their quotidian and social circumstances. Leaving behind the discourse of knowledge and mastery, they maintained, without relent and throughout the whole of their existence, a tacit relation to music. Their playing was full of habits they had cultivated since childhood and of discoveries they had made in the evolution of their tastes and passions. Ultimately, do their experiences offer us any original ideas about piano playing?

Professional players will no doubt find a certain naïveté in their discussions; they will point out the ingenuousness typical of philosophers who think they are making discoveries simply because they haven't listened to those who really know. But it is precisely the amateurism of these three philosophers that is of interest. Adorno and Jankélévitch were, no doubt, better pianists who produced informed and impressive reflections on music. They could rival musicologists when writing on Mahler or Berg, Fauré or Ravel. Their writing and their playing cohere beautifully, uniting learned culture and technical mastery. Nietzsche, Sartre, and Barthes were good pianists too, and yet their playing belongs to a different tuning altogether, for they experienced something other than the art of music. Their physical and unstable experience of music eludes conceptualization; it can only be approached at an angle. These three thinkers stepped aside from musicology in order to express in different ways certain truths about music based on their own unique playing. Barthes attempted to formalize a little philosophy of amateur playing, but he revealed much more about it when speaking about his love for Schumann. His ethics of amateurism breaks with learned and technical discourses; it involves different values and intensities that go beyond those of the sound-matter itself.

The pianistic truths suggested by Nietzsche, Sartre, and Barthes do not have the privilege of greater pertinence on the pretext that they come from theorists. Instead these truths put into play a certain complexity that arises precisely because of their failed relation to theory. They allow us to understand even better the metonymic spectrum of the piano in its relation to thought, imagination, the psyche, and sensibility. In the eighteenth century, Father Castel conceived of a piano that would join the production of colors to the production of sounds. This somewhat simplistic yet expansive idea surely speaks to the way piano keyboards can unleash scales beyond the known harmonies. The musical practice of Nietzsche, Sartre, and Barthes is not in any way exemplary, but it allows us to understand many different palpable and imaginary displacements that can mobilize other amateur practices.

The understandings [sous-entendus] and implications of musical practice are very much like the underconversations [sous-conversations] of society—whose presence Natalie Sarraute skillfully revealed underlying society chatter. A turn of phrase, an intonation, a repetition—everything is said without being said. The world of signs and sounds is made up of barely perceptible tropisms and unspeakable canvasses on which we sketch out agreements (chords) and disagreements (discords), violence and desire. This is why accompaniment—and not objectification—allows us to hear the piano's escape from learned discourse. Accompaniment is not limited to associating sounds with colors; there is much more going on here than analogy. One need only let amateur players speak for themselves in order to discover the richness of their descriptions. They are rich despite the difficulty of putting such an experience into words without having recourse to musical analysis, properly speaking. Amateur discourse conjures up layers of meaning, summaries of feelings, and mental figures—far more than reasoned arguments ever could. One such amateur player tells me that he feels like a tightrope walker, as highly tense as the line supporting him. Another evokes the sound intensity of a piece, and in doing so, he increases the number of paradigms he uses to approach it: nostalgia, but not melancholy; joy without exhilaration; refuge, but not autism; affective abandon and the pleasure of the structure. . . . Such a prolixity of figures arises from what playing of music—and in particular playing the piano, with its orchestral power—activates. Through its use of a keyboard open to unique temperaments, piano playing allows us to proliferate figures by combining feelings, rhythms, and imaginations. Language is limited to accompanying the experience of piano playing by deploying its turns and tangents. Nevertheless, multiplicity, singularity, and metaphoricity do not preclude close contact and proximity: An accompaniment is also company.

There exists an undeclared community of piano players. They don't get together in clubs, like tennis or bridge players do. Piano playing is not a recreational activity done during one's free time and then abandoned when we go back to our usual activities. Unlike a leisure activity, piano playing outstrips the time we allot to it. It inheres lastingly in our very existence—in the way we walk and see. This community of piano players cannot be recognized by any physical trait; they are not like Larry Cohen's *Invaders,* who couldn't bend their pinkies. Yet this community goes through the body—it being understood that the body is not just a thing that senses and that music is not just directed to the ears, because it requisitions other organs and other faculties. Touch, distance, movement, shifts—all these, despite their dissimilarities, configure as many styles in our habitual playing of the keyboard as we can possibly refer to. As soon as we attempt to define these behaviors, we run the risk of fixing in language what is in fact a fluid and volatile complicity. Nevertheless, the word *allure* in French seems to me to fit them well. It designates at once: a way of moving about in space ("pace"); a way of holding one's hands ("deportment"); a social behavior ("style"); and an ability to compose rhythms and to regulate one's own speed. Of course there is no one *allure* specific to pianists that we could recognize on the street. But pianists can recognize each other by a propensity to combine *allures* to greater degrees and in different ways. This unorchestrated community, which lacks any true harmony, comes about unbeknownst to its members. A friend of mine who is a historian of art, having devoted all his thought to images, told me all the same that what counts most in his life is the piano. I realize that what binds us depends perhaps on this shared yet private playing. There is a tiny paradox in sharing a certain distance from the community. We share a life that is always a little off to the side, precluding us from totally adhering to collective rhythms and their melding cadence. I believe that piano playing encourages such distancings. First, as a matter of fact, it does so through the music it makes us love. Piano playing privileges an old-fashioned or even intimist Romanticism. This had been the instrument's moment of glory. But ever since the piano has become estranged from the sound-spaces of our era. More profoundly, the regular solicitation of imaginary temporalities required by piano playing produces and encourages a letting-go of our ordinary chronometry—whence the feeling felt by those who live in music of not being at one with their own generation. They intuitively feel a secret and sustained resistance to their own times, but a disposition to times that have been freely composed. So I have now come to wonder whether there is a hidden reason for my rather long-standing attachment to the three authors discussed here. Did my interest in them come from their piano playing, even though I had not previously been aware of it? *Thus Spoke Zarathustra, Nausea, Camera Lucida*: Had these works always been for me a matter of timbre, rhythm, and touch?

Friendships, affinities, complicities . . . the relations brought about by the piano are products of a love-life that does not have love as its model. The instrument itself is the object of an attachment that can oscillate between fetishistic use and sentimental company. Nietzsche's solitude magnifies the piano: It is the object he holds to so as not to founder; it is the object to which he still clings even after having foundered. His descriptions of the pianos that accompany his New Year's eves, creative enthusiasms, or Mediterranean wanderings express an affectionate sensuality toward the instrument. Could we not say that the piano was ultimately his true company, surviving lost friendships and lost loves? When Wagner and Salomé disappointed him, Nietzsche reinvested all his energy in the keyboard. Through it he sought to transmute his life. His travels unfortunately forced him to leave his piano behind, which is by nature a sedentary friend—the downside of its amplitude. And the instruments he meets along the way cannot really replace his own. The moment of reunion with his own piano carries with it renewal and repair, for its tuning has to be found once again. One's intimacy with the instrument resembles a shared life: The pianist knows more than anyone else the way to make her piano resonate and shine, or even how to hide its weaknesses. He knows by heart the secret of its basses, the suppleness of its hammers, and its keys, which sometimes carry the marks left behind by accidents. She looks affectionately upon the ivory, yellowing with age, of this companion there for her in good times and bad.

Loves that take shape around a piano are thus indebted to the color of its sound and the warmth of its wood, which imbue the playing of music on it with certain complicities. Sartre showed us the exquisite cabrioles that unfold before the instrument. Such amorous dance takes its rhythm from the close contact in music of the players who share its figures. In front of the piano, outside of words, Sartre intuitively discovered these "sweet friendships that come into being far away from men and against them." These moments of intimacy with his mother set the tone for a psyche that eluded the language of power and the law of fathers. Music was always associated for Sartre with this relation he maintained to women and to a love that was not subject to phallic desire. The expression Barthes employed to describe a type of Racinian love, "sororal Eros," is well suited to this musical and affectionate link that, for Sartre, unified his companions at the piano: Daughter and mother were understood as sisters. Although desire was not prohibited, it unfolded in the playing of duets. Barthes wrote: "The beloved woman is a sister for whom lust is authorized and consequently appeased." Incest with a sister was a recurrent motif in the Sartrean imagination, and through his playing of music, he implicitly adumbrated a social utopia. It was thus with four-handed playing, which provided an amorous disposition defining a whole range of relations along the horizon of a shared score. The complicity required by such a sharing, whether divided or uniting, not only requires technical skill and know-how but supposes a tying together of feelings, a balancing between the interiority of each player and the constraint of mutual understanding and exterior listening. An entire tablature of feelings and attitudes exists for four-handed playing: precedence, communion, two-in-one; but also authority, rivalry, the sadomasochistic behavior of rhythms and speeds.

Barthes knew how to approach this erotics of the piano in an even more refined way, by going into identified corporealities. And it was from his own playing and tastes that he perceived this infralanguage. Following Nietzsche, he understood that declaring one's love for this or that composer was an act of self-display. Much more than a question of judgment, this type of choice engages a style of life, a sensitivity to the world, and a fundamental psychic disposition. Our imagined intimacies with certain composers define front-lines that demarcate the compatibility of our bodies. To love or detest Schumann, Chopin, Wagner, Bizet, Ravel, Schoenberg, Gillespie, or pop music constitutes declarations of love or war; they also constitute the most complete affirmation of one's being. These names serve to designate the body's existential relation to the world, to others, to times, and to spaces. Barthes discovered these discreet but nevertheless decisive realities by suggesting that musical relations are woven with beings that do not, at bottom, have names. They are unstable composites made of sounds, rhythms, colors, transformations of feeling, sensations, and images. He gave voice to these intimate corporealities that are not even figures; they are strikes, velocities, recurrences, resonances. Piano playing supposes tightening a string within the self, striking it, making it vibrate, becoming a desiring and desired body. Nietzsche, Sartre, and Barthes each accorded an important place to the body in their thought. But through their theorizations, they objectified an anonymous body—vital force, incarnated consciousness, undisciplined organism. Their body at the piano blurs conceptualizations, without for all that revealing another, intimate and private body. The body that is lived in music comes back like a wave upon their public discourses. Still, it would be too facile to designate this body as a repressed truth. The emergence of the musical body accompanies the body properly speaking more than it secretly controls it.

Piano playing conjoins suspension and engagement. A refuge, a step to the side, an exclusive passion, the musical life of the body—piano playing enables the exceptional all the while modifying the ordinary. "I decided . . . to live in music," Sartre wrote in defining his childhood choice, anxious for the absolute. He created characters for himself through ritornellos, and he unfurled amorous circles around his mother at the piano. Above all, Sartre's formulation indicates that one does not touch upon the imagination without feeling the temptation for an existence that would suddenly escape chance and vacuity. Music appears as a necessary life in which our listless, cumbersome, sweaty body is all at once given contour. Through music this body reaches perfect beauty, in accord with the maximum intensity of sound-structures, exactly in their place because they could not be anything other than themselves. The musical body seemed to Sartre a body of glory—a body of desire without want, remainder, or approximation. In-itself for-itself. This temptation is an illusion; yet Sartre maintained and sustained it. So lucid a spirit as he did so in a parodic manner, to be sure, but also with a sensual empathy for musical substance. This temptation did not fix a horizon; instead it formed in his daily routine and in those moments of recourse when Sartre went back to the piano. Did this imagination have a regulatory role? Who can say? The piano remained a necessity, an active retreat, the unique affirmation of a self who cannot be summarized into History and who cannot totally resign himself to it. There was a need for the off-beat, for the imagination, and for the feminine to be against—utterly against—society, violence, language, and revolt.

Following different rhythms and speeds, Barthes maintained this same interior displacement. Piano playing offered him a way out of codes, discourses, doxa, and the contemporary. It was a remedy for sadness, or another way to live melancholy. Barthes associated music with love, highlighting its sometimes exhilarating, sometimes pacifying effects on amorous distress. Taking Werther as his example, he extended the Romantic version of music that consoles and suggested that melody is essentially a lullaby. Not just healing and maternal, music moreover becomes a body that carries [qui porte]. The piano replays this "carrying," functioning as a musical staff [*portée*] and setting the rhythm to the musician's imagination. Playing the instrument regularly thus constitutes a reserve, in the sense of both a retreat and a resource.

Nevertheless, despite this imaginary escape or affective refuge, ordinary life remains present in our playing, which is affected by contemporary moods and rhythms. For writers and philosophers imbued with words and grammar, playing music reveals organizations other than those of signs or ideas. Through his own musical practice, Nietzsche conceived his ambition to upset the heaviness of the world. The piano was for him—more than for Sartre or Barthes—a writing table and the battle ground where he reprocessed all his passions and fought against his despairs and weaknesses. Transmuting Schumann into Wagner, pleasing Cosima, marrying Lou, becoming Mediterranean—Nietzsche played everything out on the keyboard. More than a way out, the piano was meant to allow him to save himself, by escaping incomprehension and finding salvation in the form of a hymn to life.

Deciding to live in music implies more than a metaphor that would transpose a mode of existence into a score of notes. The pianos of Sartre, Barthes, and Nietzsche show that the choice to live in music engaged their whole body, imagination, and feeling, beyond musical time. This choice accompanied their public lives, as well as the theoretical and political positions each took up in relation to their times. Their fidelity to this choice testifies to the fact that they each followed unique rhythms articulated along the cadences of the world according to their different moods and solutions. Piano playing accompanied them even when they weren't playing, because it constitutes a disposition: a receptivity to sonorous, imaginary, and unstable corporealities that go beyond meaning. It offers a distance with regard to what they called doxa, the spirit of seriousness, or herd mentality. This receptiveness allowed them to think differently about the world. They were able to set it to a different rhythm, hearing and touching it differently. The piano guided their strayings: Truly we can count them among the surveyors and inventors of side paths. They listened to their own times and discovered how to determine its meter and how to inscribe other rhythms into it by displacing values, concepts, and knowledge. Their touch becomes wanderings without shadow, roads of freedom, roaming pleasures, . . . or even fantasias, ballads, barcaroles.

ACKNOWLEDGMENTS

My thanks go to those who accompanied me on this stroll following philosophers' fingers: to Édouard Glissant, for his thinking about rhythms in the Tout-monde; to Madeleine Gobeil for the gift of her film on Sartre and Beauvoir; to Maps for her diapason; to Aliocha for his ritornellos; to Xavier for his intensities.

QUOTATIONS

Where possible, quotations have been taken from the following published translations:

Barthes, Roland. *Camera Lucida: Reflections on Photography.* Tr. Richard Howard. New York: Hill and Wang, 1981.
——. *Image, Music, Text.* Tr. Stephen Heath. New York: Hill and Wang, 1977.
——. *A Lover's Discourse: Fragments.* Tr. Richard Howard. New York: Hill and Wang, 1978.
——. *The Responsibility of Forms.* Berkeley, CA: University of California Press, 1985.

——. *Roland Barthes by Roland Barthes*. Tr. Richard Howard. Berkeley, CA: University of California Press, 1994.

de Beauvoir, Simone. "Conversations with Jean-Paul Sartre," in *Adieux: A Farewell to Sartre*. Tr. Patrick O'Brian. New York: Pantheon Books, pp.131–445.

Deleuze, Gilles, and Félix Guattari. *Thousand Plateaus*. Tr. Brian Massumi. New York: The Athlone Press, 2000.

von Goethe, Johann Wolfgang. *The Sorrows of Young Werther*. Tr. R. Dillon. Boston: Joseph Knight, 1893.

Jankélévitch, Vladimir. *Ravel*. Tr. Margaret Crosland. New York: Grove Press, 1959.

Nietzsche, Friedrich. *Beyond Good and Evil: Prelude to a Philosophy of the Future*. Ed. Rolf-Peter Horstmann. Tr Judith Norman. Cambridge: Cambridge University Press, 2002.

——. *The Birth of Tragedy and the Case of Wagner*. Tr. Walter Kaufmann. New York: Vintage Books, 1967.

——. *The Case of Wagner*, in *The Birth of Tragedy*. [The quotation from page 000 has been modified to read, "Music must be Mediterranian-ized." The quotations "Wagner is an actor . . ." and "He's a nervous breakdown . . ." are also modified.]

——. *Ecce Homo*. See *On the Genealogy of Morals and Ecce Homo*.

——. "Expeditions of an Untimely Man." in *Twilight of the Idols and The Anti-Christ*.

——. *On the Genealogy of Morals and Ecce Homo*. Tr. Walter Kaufmann. New York: Vintage Books, 1989.

——. *Twilight of the Idols and The Anti-Christ*. Tr. R. J. Hollingdale. New York: Penguin Books, 2003.

——. *The Wanderer and His Shadow*, in *Human, All Too Human: A Book for Free Spirits*. 2nd ed. Tr. R. J. Hollingdale. Cambridge: Cambridge University Press, 1996.

Sagan, Françoise. "Love Letter to Jean-Paul Sartre," in *With Fondest Regards*. Tr. Christine Donougher. London: W. H. Allen, 1986. pp. 147–59.

Sartre, Jean-Paul. "The Angel of Morbidity," in *The Writings of Jean-Paul Sartre*. Vol. 2. Eds. Michel Contat and Michel Rybalka. Tr. Richard C. McCleary. Evanston: Northwestern University Press, 1974.

——. *The Family Idiot: Gustave Flaubert, 1821–1857*. 5 Vols. Tr. Carol Cosman. Chicago: University of Chicago Press, 1981–91.

——. *Nausea*. Tr. Lloyd Alexander. New York: New Directions Books, 2007. [The quotation from page ooo has been modified to read "Dumb fucks."]

——. *The Words: The Autobiography of Jean-Paul Sartre*. Tr. Bernard Frechtman. New York: Vintage Books, 1981. [The quotation from page ooo has been modified to read "long, black hair combed in the style of Joan of Arc."]

INDEX

accompaniment (at piano), 20–21, 104, 112–13, 147–48, 150–51. *See also* four-hand piano playing

Adorno, Theodor, 3, 9, 24, 26, 75, 96–97, 146

d'Agoult, Marie, 59

amateurism, 95–98, 102–3, 106–7, 146–48

"The Angel of Morbidity" (*L'ange du morbide;* Sartre), 12

Arendt, Hannah, 75

Bach, Johann Sebastian, 27–28, 34, 51, 112

Balzac, Honoré de, 59, 60

Barcarole in F-sharp major (Chopin), 58–59, 60–61

Barthes, Roland, 2–5, 95–144, 145–47, 151–52, 154–55; and amateurism, 97–98, 102–3; childhood of, 110–11; and Chopin, 121–27, 131; as composer, 112, 132; and female companionship, 111, 113, 151; and imagination, 108, 115, 120, 142, 153–54; and *jouissance*, 114–15, 126, 135–39; and language, 135, 139–40; on listening, 115–18; and maternal relationship, 26, 111–13; and melancholy, 109, 111–12, 121, 138, 153; and modernity, 133–34, 144; musical taste of, 100, 106, 119–26, 130–35, 140; as musicologist, 96–99, 100–101, 120–21, 127–28; and Nietzsche, 122–23, 128–32; piano playing of, 96–97, 101–10, 113, 135–43, 151, 153–54; and rhythm, 106, 113, 124, 135–39, 143–44; and Romantic music, 104, 109, 112, 126–30, 138, 153; and Schumann, 3, 100, 103, 111–12, 118, 121–23, 125–32, 140–41, 144, 146; and sight-reading, 104–5, 107, 109–13; and tempo, 104–6; and temporality, 103, 106

Bartók, Béla, 126

Beaufils, Marcel, 127

Beauvoir, Simone de, 13–14, 21, 23, 32

Beethoven, Ludwig van, 51, 59, 62, 66, 83–84, 111, 129–31

Being and Nothingness (*L'être et le néant*; Sartre), 18–20
Bellini, Vincenzo, 80, 100
Benjamin, René, 75
Bercot, André, 14
Beyond Good and Evil (Nietzsche), 54, 129–30
The Birth of Tragedy (Nietzsche), 46, 56, 68, 70, 78
Bizet, Georges, 9, 55, 80–82, 131, 133
Blanchot, Maurice, 107
Bosseur, Jean-Yves, 8
Boucourechliev, André, 113
Boulez, Pierre, 120
Bourdieu, Pierre, 101
Brahms, Johannes, 73
Brooks, Shelton, 43
Bülow, Hans von, 68, 71–72
Byron, Lord, 67, 130

Callas, Maria, 100
Camera Lucida (Barthes), 108, 111–12, 122, 149
Carmen (Bizet), 80–82, 85, 86, 92
Carnaval (Schumann), 131
Carter, Andrew, 120
The Case of Wagner (Nietzsche), 73, 82
Castel, Louis-Bertrand, SJ, 147
La cause du peuple (publication), 36–37
Charpentier, Marc-Antoine, 126
Chéreau, Patrice, 127
Chopin, Frédéric-François, 12, 45, 104; Barthes and, 121–27, 131; Nietzsche and, 55–64, 81, 123; Sartre and, 3, 9–11, 15–16, 28–29, 36, 38, 44, 112
Coltrane, John, 43
composition, 148; Barthes and, 112, 132; Nietzsche and, 50, 64, 66–72, 83–84, 92, 112
Contat, Michel, 43
Copernicus, Nicolaus, 62
Couperin, François, 132
Critique of Dialectical Reason (*Critique de la raison dialectique*; Sartre), 32–34

Davidsbündlertänze (Schumann), 136–37
Davis, Miles, 43
Debussy, Claude, 1, 44, 132–33
A Defeat (*Une défaite*; Sartre), 45–47
Deleuze, Gilles, 118–19, 132
displacement, 101, 119; and piano playing, 145–46, 149, 153
Divertimento in F-Major (Barthes), 112
dreams, 23–26
dualism, 18
Dufour, Éric, 70
Dvořák, Antonin Leopold, 100

Ecce Homo (Nietzsche), 71, 73, 78, 85–86
Elkaïm, Arlette (daughter of Sartre), 2, 15–16, 20–21, 23, 44
emotion, 10, 57, 100, 102, 114, 121, 127, 135
escape, music as, 3–4, 10, 25–26, 29, 31, 44–45, 142, 152–53
existentialism, 2, 45

Fabre, Florence, 70–72
The Family Idiot (*L'idiot de la famille*; Sartre), 36
Fantasiestücke (Schumann), 136–37
Farinelli, Carlo Broschi, 118
Fauré, Gabriel-Urbain, 132
female companionship: Barthes and, 111, 113, 151; Sartre and, 20–23, 29, 150–51
Flaubert, Gustave, 10–11, 36–38, 59
Förster, Elisabeth (sister of Nietzsche), 51, 52, 64
Foucault, Michel Paul, 120
four-hand piano playing, 30, 52, 69–70, 83, 113, 151
Fragments (Nietzsche), 90
France Musique, 100, 105–6
François, Claude, 119
Freud, Sigmund, 53, 77
Friedrich, Caspar, 88

Gast, Peter (Heinrich Köselitz), 52, 53, 84–85, 88

Germanism, 55, 58, 60–62, 79, 82, 130, 133
Gersdorff, Carl von, 65, 83
Gesang der Frühe (Schumann), 112
Gide, André, 111
Goethe, Johann Wolfgang von, 118
Gould, Glenn, 126
Gracián, Baltasar, 133
"The Grain of the Voice" (Barthes), 112
Guattari, Félix, 118–19, 132

Handel, Georg Friedrich, 51, 126
hands, 18–20, 53–54
Haskil, Clara, 102
Haydn, Franz Joseph, 51, 58, 66
Hegel, Georg Wilhelm Friedrich, 75, 76
Heidegger, Martin, 133
Heine, Heinrich, 131
History, 32, 35–38, 137, 153
"How to Live Together" (seminar; Barthes), 143
Hugo, Victor, 60, 76
Hymn to Friendship (Nietzsche), 83–84
Hymn to Life (Nietzsche), 89

The Imaginary (*L'imaginaire*; Sartre), 24
imagination: Barthes and, 108, 115, 120, 142, 153–54; music and, 22, 28–29, 135, 147–48, 154; Nietzsche and, 50, 62, 66–67; Sartre and, 24–26, 28–29, 31, 35–36, 42–44, 151–53
improvisation, 64–66, 90, 92
Institute for Research and Coordination of Acoustic/Music (IRCAM), 120
Italy, 58–61, 80

Jankélévitch, Vladimir, 3, 96–97, 133, 141, 146
Janz, Curt Paul, 50
jazz, 39–44
jouissance, 114–15, 126, 135–39

Kaisermarsch (Wagner), 73
Kant, Immanuel, 77
Karlémami (grandparents of Sartre), 28
Koltès, Bernard-Marie, 127
Kosakiewicz, Wanda, 21
Köselitz, Heinrich (Peter Gast), 52, 53, 84–85, 88
Kreisleriana (Schumann), 138
Krug, Gustav, 52, 67, 70

Lagache, Daniel, 24
language: Barthes and, 135, 139–40; music and, 141–43, 148, 153–54; Nietzsche and, 52–53, 75–76, 80, 93; Sartre and, 21–22, 34, 44, 151
Lannes, Annie (cousin of Sartre), 13
Leibowitz, René, 8
Lettres d'un voyageur (Sand), 60
Libération, 37
Ligeti, György, 120
Lipatti, Dinu, 102
listening, 10, 23, 82–83, 85–86, 89, 115–18, 135
"Listening" (Barthes), 117
Liszt, Franz, 59–60, 72, 127
"Love Letter to Jean-Paul Sartre" (Sagan), 22–23
A Lover's Discourse: Fragments (Barthes), 103, 118, 125, 142
La lune blanche (Fauré), 132

Madame Bovary (Flaubert), 11, 36–38
madness, 52–53, 57, 130–31
Mancy, Anne-Marie (mother of Sartre), 21, 26–30, 32
Mancy, Joseph, 29–30, 32
Manfred (Schumann), 55, 67
Manfred-Meditation (Nietzsche), 68, 70–72, 83
Marxism, 33, 37
maternal relationships: Barthes and, 26, 111–13; Nietzsche and, 51, 62; Sartre and, 21, 26–30, 32, 151–52
Maupomé, Claude, 100, 129
Mazurka op. 7, no. I (Chopin), 64
mazurkas, 64, 123

Die Meistersinger (Wagner), 68
melancholy, 11–13, 58, 130–31, 148;
  Barthes and, 109, 111–12, 121,
  138, 153; Nietzsche and, 69–70;
  Sartre and, 11, 13, 20
Mendelssohn, Felix, 27, 30–31, 34
Merleau-Ponty, Maurice, 135
Messiaen, Olivier Eugène Prosper
  Charles, 120
Michelet, Jules, 137
modernity: Barthes and, 133–34,
  144; Nietzsche and, 73–76, 79–80,
  86, 129; Sartre and, 8, 29, 41
Mondnacht (Schumann), 131
Montaigne, Michel Eyquem de, 93,
  107
Monteverdi, Claudio, 100
Mozart, Wolfgang Amadeus, 51, 58,
  66, 121–22, 129
music: and dreams, 24–26; and
  emotion, 10, 57, 100, 102, 114,
  121, 127, 135; as escape, 3–4, 10,
  25–26, 29, 31, 44–45, 142, 152–
  53; and imagination, 22, 28–29,
  135, 147–48, 154; and language,
  141–43, 148, 153–54; and listening, 10, 23, 82–83, 85–86, 115–16,
  135; physical aspects of, 2, 4, 10,
  78, 82–83, 87–88, 103, 105, 115,
  122, 127, 135, 137; and sexuality,
  135, 137–39; and temporality,
  2–4, 10, 22–23, 35, 39, 73–75;
  and writing, 15, 41, 154. *See also*
  piano playing
musicology, 2–3, 23, 146; Barthes
  and, 96–99, 100–101, 120–21,
  127–28; Nietzsche and, 51, 55,
  81–83, 89–90; Sartre and, 8–9
Mythologies (Barthes), 127

Nachklang einer Sylvesternacht
  (*Echo of a New Year's Eve*;
  Nietzsche), 69–70
Nausea (*La nausée*; Sartre), 13–15,
  19–20, 40–42, 45, 117, 149
Nietzki family, 61
Nietzsche, Friedrich, 3–5, 49–93,
  96–97, 101, 109, 136, 143, 145–

55; and Barthes, 122–23, 128–32;
  and Bizet, 9, 80–82; and Chopin,
  55–64, 81, 123; as composer, 50,
  64, 66–72, 83–84, 92, 112; family
  of, 51–53, 62; and Germanism,
  55, 58, 60–62, 79, 82, 130; and
  imagination, 50, 62, 66–67; and
  improvisation, 64–66, 90, 92; and
  Italy, 58–61, 80; and language,
  52–53, 75–76, 80, 93; madness of,
  52–53, 57, 130; and melancholy,
  69–70; and modernity, 73–76, 79–
  80, 86, 129; musical taste of, 55,
  61, 68, 74, 81–83, 97, 122–23; and
  musicology, 51, 55, 81–83, 89–90;
  and physical body, 53–54, 78,
  82–83, 86–89, 115; piano playing
  of, 51–52, 54, 69–70, 83–84, 88,
  90–93, 113, 150, 154; and Romantic music, 9, 57, 66–72, 80, 89,
  128–30; and Salomé, 53–54, 59,
  80, 83–85, 150; and Sartre, 45–47;
  and Schumann, 55, 57, 66–70,
  81, 123, 128–31; and Wagner, 3,
  9–10, 50, 54–58, 67–82, 84, 86,
  123, 128–29, 150
Nizan, Paul, 13–14, 15
nostalgia, 26, 108, 110–11, 128, 148
Novalis (Friedrich Leopold von
  Hardenberg), 131

Ode to Joy (Beethoven), 83–84
On the Genealogy of Morals
  (Nietzsche), 61
operas, 58, 80–82, 85
operettas, 9, 28, 31
d'Orléans, Charles, 112
Overbeck, Franz, 52, 53, 62, 69

Paganini, Niccolò, 103
Panorama de la musique (journal),
  135
Panzéra, Charles Auguste Louis,
  113, 132
Parker, Charlie, 43
Parsifal (Wagner), 77, 82
Pelléas et Mélisande (Debussy), 132
Philip V (of Spain), 118

photography, 98, 108, 121–22, 140
physical body: music and, 2, 4, 10, 78, 82–83, 87–88, 103, 105, 115, 122, 127, 135, 137; Nietzsche and, 53–54, 78, 82–83, 86–89; piano playing and, 17–20, 105, 107–8, 115, 140–41, 145–46, 148, 151–54
piano (instrument), 3, 52, 101, 150
piano playing: and accompaniment, 20–21, 104, 112–13, 147–48, 150–51; of Barthes, 96–97, 101–10, 113, 135–43, 151, 153–54; and displacement, 145–46, 149, 153; four-hand, 30, 52, 69–70, 83, 113, 151; of Nietzsche, 51–52, 54, 69–70, 83–84, 88, 90–93, 113, 150, 154; physical aspects of, 17–20, 105, 107–8, 115, 140–41, 145–46, 148, 151–54; of Sartre, 15–21, 25–26, 30, 44, 47, 106, 108–9, 113, 150–51; and technical mastery, 102, 105–8, 114, 128, 146, 151; and temporality, 98, 148–49; and thought, 102–3, 135, 147, 154–55; and touch, 18–20, 105, 135–36, 148
"Piano-souvenir" (Barthes), 110
Pousseur, Henri, 120
Prayer to Life (Nietzsche), 84
"Prayer to Life" (Salomé), 84
Proust, Marcel, 101
public vs. private, 2–4, 10, 35–36, 68
I Puritani (Bellini), 100

Querelle des Bouffons (Quarrel of the Comic Actors), 81

Ravel, Maurice, 104, 132–33
Rebeyrol, Philippe, 112
Rée, Paul, 53, 84
rhythm: Barthes and, 106, 113, 124, 135–39, 143–44; Nietzsche and, 91–92; Sartre and, 20, 28, 32–33
Richter, Hans, 124
Riedel, Carl, 84
Rilke, Rainer Maria, 53
Der Ring des Nibelungen (The Ring of the Nibelung; Wagner), 73

Ritschl, Friedrich Wilhelm, 67
Rohde, Erwin, 52, 83
Roland Barthes by Roland Barthes, 108, 115–16, 121, 126
Romanticism, 13, 34, 47, 57–60, 86, 88, 140, 149
Romantic music, 149; Barthes and, 104, 109, 112, 126–30, 138, 153; Nietzsche and, 9, 57, 66–72, 80, 89, 128–30; Sartre and, 3, 9–16, 41, 44
Rossini, Gioacchino Antonio, 80
Rousseau, Jean-Jacques, 3, 96–97, 130
Rubinstein, Arthur, 124, 126

Sagan, Françoise, 22–23, 126
Salomé, Lou, 53–54, 59, 80, 83–85, 150
Sand, George, 11, 59–60
Sarraute, Natalie, 147
Sartre, Jean-Paul, 1–5, 7–47, 116, 126, 134–35, 143, 145–55; childhood of, 22, 26–32; and Chopin, 3, 9–11, 15–16, 28–29, 36, 38, 44, 112; and drug use, 24–25, 32–33; and female companionship, 20–23, 150–51; and Flaubert, 10–11, 36–38; and imagination, 24–26, 28–29, 31, 35–36, 42–44, 151–53; and jazz, 39–44; and language, 21–22, 34, 44, 151; and maternal relationship, 21, 26–30, 32, 151–52; and melancholy, 11, 13, 20; and modernity, 8, 29, 41; musical taste of, 28, 40, 44, 97; as musicologist, 8–9; and Nietzsche, 45–47; piano playing of, 15–21, 25–26, 30, 44, 47, 106, 108–9, 113, 150–51; and rhythm, 20, 28, 32–33; and Romantic music, 3, 9–16, 41, 44; and sight-reading, 16–17, 40; and temporality, 22–23, 33, 35–39; writing style of, 33–35
Satie, Erik, 126, 133
Schiller, Ferdinand Canning Scott, 130

Schoenberg, Arnold Franz Walter, 8, 44
Schopenhauer, Arthur, 50
Schubert, Franz Peter, 59, 100, 111
Schumann, Robert Alexander, 119, 136; Barthes and, 3, 100, 103, 111–12, 118, 121–23, 125–32, 140–41, 144, 146; Nietzsche and, 55, 57, 66–70, 81, 123, 128–31
Schweitzer, Albert, 27, 46
Schweitzer, Charles, 26–27, 30–32
Schweitzer, Louis Théophile, 27
Schweitzer family, 13, 28, 40, 46
sexuality, 135, 137–39
Shelley, Percy Bysshe, 118
Sicard, Michel, 8
sight-reading: Barthes and, 104–5, 107, 109–13; Nietzsche and, 64; Sartre and, 16–17, 40
Six Concert Études on Caprices by Paganini (Schumann), 103–4
Socrates, 77
"Some of These Days" (Brooks), 40–43, 117
Sonatine (Ravel), 132
Stendhal (Marie-Henri Beyle), 60
Stockhausen, Karlheinz, 120
the Superman (Nietzsche), 61, 88
Eine Sylvesternacht (A New Year's Eve; Nietzsche), 69

taste, musical, 3, 45, 96–97, 151–52; of Barthes, 100, 106, 119–26, 130–35, 140; of Nietzsche, 55, 61, 68, 74, 81–83, 97, 122–23; of Sartre, 28, 40, 44, 97
technical mastery, 16, 102, 105–8, 114, 128, 146, 151
tempo, 90–91, 104–6, 148–49
temporality: Barthes and, 103, 106; music and, 2–4, 10, 22–23, 35, 39, 73–75; piano playing and, 98,

148–49; Sartre and, 22–23, 33, 35–39
thought: and listening, 82–83, 85–86, 89, 115; and piano playing, 102–3, 135, 147, 154–55
Thousand Plateaus (Deleuze and Guattari), 132
Thus Spoke Zarathustra (Nietzsche), 50, 85–88, 149
time. See temporality
totalitarianism, 75–76
touch, 18–20, 105, 135–36, 148
Tristan (Wagner), 68, 70, 71
Triumphlied (Brahms), 73
Twilight of the Gods (Wagner), 74
Twilight of the Idols (Nietzsche), 60, 73–74
Twombly, Cy, 106

Vian, Boris, 43
Vian, Michelle, 21, 43
Vivaldi, Antonio, 126
Von Meysenbug, Malwida, 54

Wagner, Cosima, 45–46, 59, 67–72
Wagner, Richard, 43, 45–46, 131, 133; Nietzsche and, 3, 9–10, 50, 54–58, 67–82, 84, 86, 123, 128–29, 150
The Wanderer and His Shadow (Nietzsche), 56
Webern, Anton Friedrich Wilhelm von, 44, 100, 120
The Well-Tempered Clavier (Bach), 112
Wittgenstein, Ludwig Josef Johan, 77, 96–97
Wittgenstein, Paul, 104
The Words (Les mots; Sartre), 2, 14, 26, 116

Zarathustra, 62, 80, 131

EUROPEAN PERSPECTIVES

A Series in Social Thought and Cultural Criticism

Lawrence D. Kritzman, Editor

Gilles Deleuze	*The Logic of Sense*
Julia Kristeva	*Strangers to Ourselves*
Theodor W. Adorno	*Notes to Literature*, vols. 1 and 2
Richard Wolin, editor	*The Heidegger Controversy*
Antonio Gramsci	*Prison Notebooks*, vols. 1, 2, and 3
Jacques LeGoff	*History and Memory*
Alain Finkielkraut	*Remembering in Vain: The Klaus Barbie Trial and Crimes Against Humanity*
Julia Kristeva	*Nations Without Nationalism*
Pierre Bourdieu	*The Field of Cultural Production*
Pierre Vidal-Naquet	*Assassins of Memory: Essays on the Denial of the Holocaust*
Hugo Ball	*Critique of the German Intelligentsia*
Gilles Deleuze	*Logic and Sense*
Gilles Deleuze and Félix Guattari	*What Is Philosophy?*
Karl Heinz Bohrer	*Suddenness: On the Moment of Aesthetic Appearance*
Julia Kristeva	*Time and Sense: Proust and the Experience of Literature*
Alain Finkielkraut	*The Defeat of the Mind*
Julia Kristeva	*New Maladies of the Soul*
Elisabeth Badinter	*XY: On Masculine Identity*
Karl Löwith	*Martin Heidegger and European Nihilism*
Gilles Deleuze	*Negotiations, 1972–1990*
Pierre Vidal-Naquet	*The Jews: History, Memory, and the Present*
Norbert Elias	*The Germans*
Louis Althusser	*Writings on Psychoanalysis: Freud and Lacan*
Elisabeth Roudinesco	*Jacques Lacan: His Life and Work*
Ross Guberman	*Julia Kristeva Interviews*
Kelly Oliver	*The Portable Kristeva*
Pierre Nora	*Realms of Memory: The Construction of the French Past* vol. 1: *Conflicts and Divisions* vol. 2: *Traditions* vol. 3: *Symbols*
Claudine Fabre-Vassas	*The Singular Beast: Jews, Christians, and the Pig*
Paul Ricoeur	*Critique and Conviction: Conversations with François Azouvi and Marc de Launay*
Theodor W. Adorno	*Critical Models: Interventions and Catchwords*
Alain Corbin	*Village Bells: Sound and Meaning in the Nineteenth-Century French Countryside*
Zygmunt Bauman	*Globalization: The Human Consequences*
Emmanuel Levinas	*Entre Nous: Essays on Thinking-of-the-Other*
Jean-Louis Flandrin and Massimo Montanari	*Food: A Culinary History*

Tahar Ben Jelloun   *French Hospitality: Racism and North African Immigrants*

Emmanuel Levinas   *Alterity and Transcendence*

Sylviane Agacinski   *Parity of the Sexes*

Alain Finkielkraut   *In the Name of Humanity: Reflections on the Twentieth Century*

Julia Kristeva   *The Sense and Non-Sense of Revolt: The Powers and Limits of Psychoanalysis*

Régis Debray   *Transmitting Culture*

Catherine Clément   *The Feminine and the Sacred*
and Julia Kristeva

Alain Corbin   *The Life of an Unknown: The Rediscovered World of a Clog Maker in Nineteenth-Century France*

Michel Pastoureau   *The Devil's Cloth: A History of Stripes and Striped Fabric*

Julia Kristeva   *Hannah Arendt*

Carlo Ginzburg   *Wooden Eyes: Nine Reflections on Distance*

Elisabeth Roudinesco   *Why Psychoanalysis?*

Alain Cabantous   *Blasphemy: Impious Speech in the West from the Seventeenth to the Nineteenth Century*

Luce Irigaray   *Between East and West: From Singularity to Community*

Julia Kristeva   *Melanie Klein*

Gilles Deleuze   *Dialogues II*

Julia Kristeva   *Intimate Revolt: The Powers and Limits of Psychoanalysis, vol. 2*

Claudia Benthien   *Skin: On the Cultural Border Between Self and the World*

Sylviane Agacinski   *Time Passing: Modernity and Nostalgia*

Emmanuel Todd   *After the Empire: The Breakdown of the American Order*

Hélène Cixous   *Portrait of Jacques Derrida as a Young Jewish Saint*

Gilles Deleuze   *Difference and Repetition*

Gianni Vattimo   *Nihilism and Emancipation: Ethics, Politics, and Law*

Julia Kristeva   *Colette*

Steve Redhead, editor   *The Paul Virilio Reader*

Roland Barthes   *The Neutral: Lecture Course at the Collège de France (1977–1978)*

Gianni Vattimo   *Dialogue with Nietzsche*

Gilles Deleuze   *Nietzsche and Philosophy*

Hélène Cixous   *Dream I Tell You*

Jacques Derrida   *Geneses, Genealogies, Genres, and Genius: The Secrets of the Archive*

Jean Starobinski   *Enchantment: The Seductress in Opera*

Julia Kristeva   *This Incredible Need to Believe*

Marta Segarra, editor   *The Portable Cixous*

François Dosse   *Gilles Deleuze and Félix Guattari: Intersecting Lives*

Julia Kristeva   *Hatred and Forgiveness*

Antoine de Baecque   *History/Cinema*